Heroes All

Amazing Stories of World War II

Elbert L. Watson

Traveler Enterprises
Easley, SC

Faith Printing Co.

Taylors, SC

ISBN 978-1-4675-1200-8

Watson, Elbert L., 1930—

HEROES ALL, AMAZING STORIES OF WORLD WAR II.

Includes bibliographical references.

ELBERT L. WATSON is a former publisher of military history and the author of three other books and numerous historical articles in professional journals. Now retired he lives in Easley, South Carolina.

The author gratefully acknowledges the assistance of Brett Looper in the preparation of the text, and also thanks Juanita Barnett for preparing the cover of the book.

Printed in the United States of America.

For Alex Vraciu
"Hellcat" of an ace

Contents

Introduction

In August 1945 my father, Elbert L. Watson, Sr., was transferred from Camp Barkley, Texas, to the West Coast. There he would await orders to participate in the expected land invasion of Japan. He knew, as did thousands of other young men around him, that Japan, under tight military control, was preparing to commit national suicide against an invading force, regardless of its size. No doubt about it, a blood-bath lay ahead for America and her allies. Very likely, Normandy's D-Day would pale in comparison.

Fortunately, at that critical moment, while my father and his buddies stood, perhaps, on the brink of eternity, two atomic bombs broke free from the bomb bay doors of two powerful B-29s, soaring high above the Japanese cities of Hiroshima and Nagasaki. Following those missions, the horror of World War II came to an abrupt and decisive end several days later. My father never had to climb aboard that troopship. Instead, he returned in one piece to our home in Birmingham, Alabama. During the extra years given him, he plied his trade as a leather salesman; sang a rich baritone in his church choir; and, oh yes, was a vocal backer of Alabama's vaunted Crimson Tide. He lived a full life, finally passing away in 1988.

As a young fellow just turning 15, the stirring events back then obviously made a profound and lasting impression on me. Early on, I realized how fortunate I was that my father "actually" survived World War II. Thousands of other youngsters were not so lucky: they lost their dads in such places as Normandy, Guadalcanal, Iwo Jima, Hurtegen Forest, Okinawa---or in disease infested prison camps.

So here I am in the latter years of my own life, pondering what ultimately was required to get my father home safely. Was it "just" the dropping of two powerful, destructive bombs? Hardly! Think of all the blood and sweat that preceded those two epic events: the islands that fell to the Marines; the crude airfields that were scooped out by the Seabees; the fiery sea battles that were fought and won by the Navy; and the great bombing raids that were carried out by the Army Air Corps! You see, many thousands of unknown soldiers, sailors, and marines played major roles in bringing my dad home.

Heroes All is written with the general reader in mind. Well aware of the possible fate that awaited my father, I have focused on events in the Pacific Theatre with these much too brief accounts. Too, it should be noted, that much of what took place in the Pacific directly impacted on American strategy in Europe. For instance, had we lost at Midway in 1942, would there have been a Normandy two years later?

Of course, the extraordinary courage manifested by our fighting forces was not restricted to one place during the war, nor to the men on the front lines. There were chaplains, athletes, even animals who contributed to the final victory. They deserve to be remembered, as well. Though these exciting accounts provide little more than snapshots of what happened high aloft, on the high seas, or across fiery battlefields, several of them raise questions that, hopefully, will encourage the reader to explore the subjects in much more detail.

As indicated, *Heroes All* focuses on breath-taking air missions that were carried out with split second timing, most of them performed deep within Japanese held territory. Had our forces failed in those brief moments when faced with either success or failure, much of what occurred later on the sea and ground (mostly small islands), never would have happened, or, at best, been seriously curtailed. Is it too audacious to suggest that the Pacific phase of World War II was ultimately decided by mere seconds? Let the reader decide.

I am indebted to many fine folks who encouraged me in this project. My personal acquaintance with many outstanding veterans has, in a real sense, lifted the curtain for me to understand, if only vaguely, how one felt to be out there on the point during the war. Some of these men whose stories appear in this book include Paul Tibbets, George Gay, Adrian Marks, Robert Palmer, Alex Vraciu, and former President George H.W. Bush. All of these men (the first four are now deceased) provided me with material, photos, or interviews. My sincere thanks to all of them.

Finally, I am grateful to my wife Ramona who has been a constant source of encouragement for me to see the project through to its end.

Elbert L. Watson

Easley, South Carolina, November 2011

Chapter I

Doolittle's Raid: *Payback for Pearl Harbor*

No doubt about it, America's back was to the wall in early 1942 following Japan's ruthless assault on Pearl Harbor. Our Pacific Fleet was virtually wiped out; Guam and Wake Island were gone; and the outlook in the Philippines was bleak at best. Even our west coast shores appeared vulnerable to attack. Americans were rightly nervous. Where would Japan strike next?

Never had America's national security been in such dire straits. We were pummeled but not down. Ours was a proud country. A day of retribution would surely come. But how— and when? To delay an early response raised the possibility that the patriotic euphoria currently sweeping the country would be muted. Young men were swarming to the draft boards as "Remember Pearl Harbor" became our rallying cry. Though things looked bad, home front morale was very high. Still, Americans expected our leaders to strike back soon against Japan, very soon.

No person agreed with them more than did President Franklin D. Roosevelt, who was painfully aware that it was on his watch that the country had sustained such a humiliating defeat by the surprise attack. Historians today regard Roosevelt as one of our most astute politicians, crediting him with having a unique ability to mold and manipulate public opinion. But Roosevelt was also brainy and smart enough to surround himself with brilliant, incisive military thinkers. Included in his inner circle were Secretary of the Navy Frank Knox; Army Chief of Staff, George C. Marshall; Commander in Chief U.S. Fleet, Ernest J. King; and Army Air Corps Chief of Staff, Henry A. "Hap" Arnold.

Seen here during his barnstorming days, Jimmie Doolittle captured all of the top racing trophies during aviation's pioneer days.

It was in the lap of this headstrong and disparate group of men, that Roosevelt placed the grave responsibility of devising a way to take the war all the way to the Japanese mainland. "Use your imaginations," he urged. With their orders clearly spelled out, these men (the forerunners of the Joint Chiefs of Staff) began meeting regularly in the second-floor White House library-office. Joining them were presidential assistant Harry Hopkins and General Edwin Watson, military aide to the president.

Marshall and King dominated the secret sessions. Numerous ideas were brought forward, discussed, evaluated, and then dropped. With America clearly on the defensive, an overly ambitious idea appeared incredulous at the moment. A bombing raid obviously was the most practical and dramatic way to show America's home front and, indeed, the world, that Japan would pay a heavy price for her heinous attack at Hawaii.

But the big question was how to do it! Sure, long range bombers could be transferred to air bases in China, our ally, from where they could be launched against Japanese industrial centers. Though a sensible idea, it was not practical because of the real possibility of a "leak." Close-range navy fighters and small bombers made up carrier air power and were a possibility, but if U.S. ships got too near Japan they would be vulnerable to attack and destruction by enemy defense forces. America simply could not sustain another disaster like the one that happened at Pearl Harbor. There must be a better way. But time was running out. A defining moment was at hand. Was there such a thing as a miracle on the near horizon?

Captain Low has a brainstorm

Apparently there was! On Sunday, January 10, 1942, Captain Francis Low, King's operational officer, was in Norfolk, Virginia, to observe the navy's latest aircraft carrier, *USS Hornet,* going through its shakedown cruise in preparation for service in the Pacific. As he awaited takeoff for the trip back to Washington that afternoon, Low, who had sat in on several of the secret meetings, randomly looked out the window and noticed that an adjoining airfield was laid out in the dimensions of an aircraft carrier's flight deck, in order to assist the navy's young trainees with their carrier landings and takeoffs.

That in itself was nothing new to Low, but what happened next caused a light bulb to go off in his head. Just at that moment two fat bellied army bombers had no problem landing on the fake carrier deck. Could the same feat be carried out on the flight deck of an actual carrier? It was a thought worth exploring during his short trip home.

Back in Washington, Low wasted no time button-holing King in the admiral's flagship *Vixen* that was anchored in the nearby Anacostia River. After carefully making his point, he held his breath while King took a few moments to reflect on the ambitious idea. Finally, the crusty old admiral leaned forward and quietly replied that the idea just might work. Low was instructed to see Captain Donald B. Duncan, King's air operation's officer, and report back.

At first Duncan was skeptical. O.K. it might be possible for small twin-engineered bombers to fly off a carrier's deck, but how, he pointedly asked, could they land on it once the mission was completed. Their weak "bellies" could not adapt to arrester hooks, so that idea was out. Still, it might be possible for the planes to land elsewhere, or even ditched in the ocean where destroyers would pick up surviving crew members.

Concluding that the bold idea was technically possible, the two men reported back to a receptive King on January 16. He enthusiastically told them to go full throttle with their plan and run it by "Hap" Arnold. Unknown to Low and Duncan, Arnold had been informed during a Christmas Eve conversation with his English counterpart, Air Marshal Charles Portal, that Britain had successfully launched torpedo planes from a carrier at Taranto and sunk three Italian battleships. Not surprisingly, Arnold was an easy convert to the idea.

Thus, as a result of mental tenacity, technical acumen, and just a plain old Yankee "go for broke" attitude, the basic idea for making a daring, if not impossible, strike against Japan's heartland was hatched in the minds of only three men in the confines of a small library room. Still to be determined was how they would find a person who had the inspirational leadership and unquestioned loyalty to implement and successfully carry out the mission.

Jimmie Doolittle takes command of the project

That man would be non-other than Lieutenant-Colonel James Harold "Jimmie" Doolittle, whose office, incredibly, was only a few doors down the hall from Arnold's. Indeed, the "Man and the Hour" had met.

Doolittle was already a household name to Americans with his impeccable aviation credentials and aerial feats. Born in Alameda, California, on December 14, 1896, the daring, driven, and incredibly brilliant Doolittle was a World War I army pilot, who had served 10 years after the war as a major in the Army Air Corps Reserve. Later turning to aerobatics, a popular past time of early aviation enthusiasts, his aerial feats included making the first trans-continental flight in 1922 from Pablo Beach, Florida to San Diego in less than 24 hours (his time was 21 hours, 19 minutes); first person to execute an outside loop; and first person to win all major aviation racing trophies.

But Doolittle was much more than a flying stunt man.

In 1923 he had graduated from the Massachusetts Institute of Technology (MIT) with a Ph D in aeronautical engineering.

A loyal patriot, Doolittle signed up in the Army Air Corps as a major as war clouds gathered in the 1930s. Promoted to lieutenant colonel, his assignment to Arnold's office set the stage for "Doolittle's Raid," the World War II saga that will forever bear his name.

Doolittle had no trouble getting the gist of what the country faced at that critical moment in the war. The plan that eventually emerged to bomb Japan was basically his and Duncan's: Doolittle representing the army and Duncan the navy. Once that was affirmed, they had to find a bomber capable of taking off from a carrier; fly approximately 2400 miles to reach prearranged airfields in eastern China; and carry a 2000 pound bomb load to drop on Tokyo and other Japanese cities. There were two possibilities: the Martin B-26 *Marauder* and the North American B-25 *Mitchell,* both of them medium bombers. Based on its superior takeoff performance the *Mitchell* got the nod.

A Happy-go-Lucky group of Raiders prepares to bomb Tokyo.

Doolittle's task was to make adjustments to the planes that would participate in the mission. Since the raid would be made at low level flying, it was necessary to remove the retractable ventral turret in order to reduce the plane's weight by approximately 600 pounds. The aircraft's total fuel load of 1141 gallons was distributed as follows: 646 gallons in the wing tanks, 225 gallons in the bomb bay tank, 160 gallons in a collapsible tank located in the crawlspace above the bomb bay, and 160 gallons in the ventral turret space. Also included were ten 5-gallon cans for refills.

The still top secret Norden bombsight, that would later play a major role in America's bombing missions across Europe and the Pacific, was removed to make sure the Japanese did not get their hands on it. Interestingly, the replacement bombsight turned out to be more effective for low level flying. The total bomb load for each plane consisted of four 500 pound bombs. Thus, Special Aviation Project No.1 was born almost purely by accident and hatched in the minds of only a few individuals!

All parties involved in the project agreed that Doolittle was the man to head up the mission. The critical question remaining was how to find a bunch of guys who could successfully carry it out.

In the end, the selection proved quite simple. The only B-25s in service during the early months of 1942 were flown by the 17th Bombardment Group, composed of the 34th, 37th, and 95th Squadrons, along with the 89th Reconnaissance Squadron. Originally based in Pendleton, Oregon, this crack unit of devil-may-care airmen had recently been transferred to Lexington Field near Columbia, South Carolina, to carry out patrol duty on the east coast. Volunteers from the unit responded overwhelmingly, despite the fact that the men had no clue as to what the mission was all about. Barely out of their teens, the fellows were eager to take the fight directly to the enemy, whether it was Japan or Germany. Enough men signed on to man 24 of the airplanes. Each plane would carry a five man crew.

The *Mitchells* selected for the mission were sent to Mid-Continent Airlines in Minneapolis, Minnesota, where necessary modifications were made on the planes. Once that was out of the way, they were flown by the crews down to Eglin Field in the Florida

Panhandle. There the men were given three weeks of intensive training in carrier deck takeoffs (on land), low level flying, over water navigation, and low altitude bombing. It was a big order, indeed, but the fellows were quite up to the task.

On March 3 Doolittle for the first time met directly with the pilots and their crews in the Eglin Operations Office, a cramped, sweaty little enclosure that was much too small for the crowd that gathered there to hear, hopefully, what the mysterious mission was all about. They learned very little. Standing erect at the front of the room, Doolittle spoke clearly and distinctly for two minutes: "My name's Doolittle. I've been put in charge of the project that you men have volunteered for. This is the toughest training you'll ever have. It will be the most dangerous thing any of you have ever done."

Cautioning them not to even try to guess what the upcoming mission was all about, he advised them to talk to no one, not even their wives or among themselves. Should any fellow get too nosy, he would be reported immediately to the FBI. Then he closed on a somber note: "If any of you have any doubts, drop out now. Any man can drop out and nothing will ever be said about it. No one will ask any questions; no one will think less of you for it."

No one was about to back out after coming under the spell of such an authentic American legend as Jimmie Doolittle. To a man they agreed to follow him anywhere, everywhere.

After completing their short training period at Eglin, the *Mitchell* crews hopped aboard their planes on March 25, revved up the engines, and flew out to the west coast. After making a brief stop at McClellan Field near Sacramento for a final checkup, they continued on up to Alameda Naval Air Station on the San Francisco Bay, landing there, ironically, on April Fool's Day. Cranes then hoisted 16 of the planes aboard the new carrier *Hornet.*

With a displacement weight of 19,800 tons and a length just slightly under 810 feet, the big carrier had already proven its mettle. On February 2, under tight security, off the coast of Norfolk, Virginia, two Mitchell medium bombers were launched from her deck. The visionary Captain Low was proven right! No question about it, Japan was now in America's

The scene aboard HORNET as Doolittle's Raiders readied themselves for take-off from the carrier's pitching deck in rough weather. U.S. Navy Photo.

crosshairs. Getting the job done was all that remained.

Later that day **Hornet** was tugged out to the middle of San Francisco Bay. Joined by several smaller ships the next morning, the carrier wasted no time heading out to the high seas. Once the "City by the Bay" had faded beyond the distant horizon, Doolittle called the men together and tersely outlined the mission for the first time. Mincing no words, he warned them that their chances of returning back were quite slim, offering them a final opportunity to back out. Both excitement and apprehension rippled through the veins of each man who stood there that day. Sure, they were anxious to take the fight to the Japanese, but as pragmatists they were fully aware of the heavy odds facing them. Still, not one man backed out.

Hornet was skippered by Admiral Marc Mitscher, a chain-smoking, crusty old naval veteran whose heavily creased face made him appear older than his age of 54. Back in 1919 he had made a trans-Atlantic flight in a navy plane, the first person to do so. Tall and spare in appearance, the sun-burned Mitscher had painted "REMEMBER PEARL HARBOR" on the carrier's stack. Obviously he meant business, as well.

When **Hornet** was two days out to sea, Mitscher bluntly announced over loud speakers and semaphoring (signaling with two flags) to the other ships the nature of the mission.. "The target of this task force is Tokyo," he bellowed out. "The army is going to bomb Japan, and we're going to get them as close to the enemy as we can. This is a chance for all of us to give the Japs a dose of their own medicine." His electrifying words were like magic. Cries of excitement arose from the various ships, as leather

Ted Lawson (left), pilot of RUPTERED DUCK and members of his crew, Dean Davenport, co-pilot, Charles McClure, Robert Clever, and David Thatcher.

tough marines and sailors alike jumped up and down, some of them crying with joy. God be praised! They would be the ones to avenge Pearl Harbor. Some wag even came up with a little ditty straight out of the "Snow White" movie: "Heigh-ho! Heigh-ho! We're off to Tokyo! We'll bomb and blast and come back fast. Heigh-ho! Heigh-ho!"

Raiders launch despite poor weather conditions

On April 10 **Hornet** joined up with another great carrier **Enterprise** to form Task Force 16, an armada of carriers, cruisers, oilers, and destroyers, the greatest naval force America had ever put together up to then. Headed up by Admiral William A. "Bull" Halsey, the fleet's goal was to get within 400 miles of Japan before launching the bombers. Should the ships be spotted by the enemy, the planes were to launch immediately and the ships withdrawn to safer waters. This was not the time for our wounded navy to take on Japan's superior naval force in an open water fight.

On the morning of April 18, Task Force 16, 300 miles short of its intended launch point, was spotted by a

Japanese patrol boat, which was quickly sunk. Almost immediately **Hornet's** public address system blared out for the men to grab their personal effects and rush to their planes. Though the planes carried enough fuel to get them to their targets, their prospects of reaching their temporary landing strips in China appeared quite bleak. There was an additional problem: the ocean had become increasingly choppy, causing **Hornet** to rise and fall on giant waves that cascaded about and over the ship's flight deck. Despite the unsatisfactory conditions, the launch could not be delayed another moment.

Doolittle himself took over the controls of bomber number one, just as a drenching rain and bitter crosswinds further complicated the already intolerable situation. Gale like winds blew directly into the plane's windshield. With every eye on Doolittle, time seemed to stand still. Finally, the checkered flag went down, Doolittle's feet came up from the brakes, and the heavily loaded **Mitchell** began its short trip down the 467 foot runway.

The pilots of the 15 remaining planes watched closely, breathlessly, and prayerfully as Doolittle inched forward. In the second plane, pilot Dick Cole thought if the Boss didn't make it, no one else would: they would simply drop into the water and that would be that. Pilot Ted Lawson, with his hawk like gaze, wondered if the strong wind would abort the mission. But Doolittle was quite up to the task facing him. Slowly picking up speed, he held the plane to the white line running down the center of the deck. Just as a powerful wave raised **Hornet's** bow up and on top of it, he gracefully lifted the bomber off with yards to spare. For a few anxious moments he hung the B-25 almost straight up, leveled off, then circled around and flew directly over the carrier to resounding cheers from fellows lining the decks.

Thus emboldened, the other pilots followed suit and were all airborne within an hour. Short though it was, their intensive training had paid off. In all the lofty annals of flight, they were the first to fly a bomber off the deck of a carrier out on the high seas—and dangerous ones at that! They had proven their mettle as pilots.

Once they were in the air, the planes at first flew 100 or so feet above the water to avoid detection. Later they split up and headed toward their respective targets.

When they arrived over Honshu, Japan's main island, the day was bright and sunny. In all, four cities were struck from altitudes of approximately 1500 feet. Ten sites were hit in Tokyo; two in Yokohama; and one in Kobe, Yokosuka, Osaka, and Nagoya. Taking hits were steelworks, warehouses, oil refineries, docks, powder and manufacturing plants, and aircraft, truck, and tank factories.

Though the Doolittle Fleet had been spotted, the Japanese were not expecting anything like this. Consequently, there was only light resistance. Ed Horton, the tail gunner on plane No. 10, recalled coming in on the north side of Tokyo Bay and experiencing light anti-aircraft fire from a carrier and other ships in the Bay. Two Japanese fighters came up and flew alongside his plane but surprisingly did not fire. He assumed they were only on training flights. Though the antiaircraft fire was minimal, Horton, like the others, was glad when the brief mission was over and they could fly out into the sea and head for the mainland of China.

Once their work was over, 15 of the planes flew southwest along the southern coast of Japan and across the East China Sea, trying to reach safe havens in China. One aircraft running low on fuel veered off toward nearby Russia. Having launched early and from a range quite beyond the acceptable safe distance necessary to reach their landing strips, each plane was practically running on fumes as night approached. Too, a strong headwind drastically impeded their progress. Could any man survive these heavy odds?

Eleven of the crews were forced to bail out; four **Mitchells** crash landed (three men died); and one plane limped into Russia. All 16 planes were lost. Eight men were captured by the Japanese: Dean Hallmark, Bill Farrow, Harold Spatz, Chase Nielson, George Barr, Bob Hite, Jacob DeShazer, and Bob Meder. Farrow, Spatz, and Hallmark were subsequently tried as war criminals and executed. The crew that landed in Russia was taken into custody and later released. Though it was allied with the United States, Russia still maintained a peace treaty with Japan at that time.

Eighty extraordinary men had put their young lives on the line for their country. Miraculously 64 of them survived the ordeal and would fight again during the war.

Solid accomplishments of the raid

Though the actual damage inflicted on the Japanese cities was quite minimal, the psychological effect that erupted on America's home front and within the military establishment was indescribable. Yankee ingenuity had made a bold statement to the Japanese that their ultimate day of reckoning lay ahead. The impact of the raid on the Empire was also quite dramatic. Confused over the point of origin of the bombers, Japan's military leaders postponed sending fighter planes and anti-aircraft guns from their home

The men who survived the mission experienced both joy and sorrow as the following examples reveal. Jimmie Doolittle returned back to America to receive a well deserved hero's welcome. At the White House the President pinned the Medal of Honor on him. During the course of his World War II career, he received two Distinguished Service Medals, the Silver Star, three Distinguished Flying Crosses, Bronze Star, and four Air Medals. Military decorations were also bestowed on him from China, Great Britain, Belgium, France, Poland, and Ecuador.

Generals Hap Arnold and George Marshal witness President Roosevelt presenting Doolittle with the Medal of Honor in a brief White House ceremony. Also seen is wife "Joe" Doolittle.

bases to forward positions in the Pacific in case of another attack.

President Roosevelt cleverly added to the confusion by casually remarking that the raiders had flown out from a secret base on an island called "Shangri-La," the mythical paradise in the Tibetan mountains written about by author James Hilton in his popular 1931 novel ***Lost Horizon.*** Japanese officials couldn't figure that one out, so they actually sent out a few search parties to find the elusive "Shangri-La."

As a brigadier-general, he commanded the 12th Air Force in North Africa, and as a major-general the North African Strategic Air Forces. By the end of the war he had risen to the rank of lieutenant-general.

Admired and respected throughout his long and useful life, Doolittle held many important posts: vice-president of Shell Oil Company; special assistant to the Air Force Chief of Staff, thus making him a key player in the early missile and space programs; and chairman of the Board of Space Technology. In

1989 President George H.W. Bush awarded him the Presidential Medal of Freedom. Doolittle flew his final mission on September 27, 1993, at the age of 93. "Joe," his beloved wife of 71 years, preceded him in death in1988. Fittingly, they are buried side by side in Section 7-A of Arlington National Cemetery.

Ted Lawson, pilot of **The Ruptured Duck,** spotted the small island of Nantien just off the coast of China and tried to land on the beach. Badly injured when he was forced to ditch in the water, it was necessary to amputate his left leg several days later because of massive infection.

One year later Lawson turned his near tragedy into a triumph, when he and the noted newspaper columnist Bob Considine collaborated together to write the 1943 best seller **Thirty Seconds Over Tokyo,** giving a dramatic and personal account of the mission. Hollywood quickly got into the act and produced a major film in 1944 by the same title. The noted actor Spencer Tracy played Doolittle and Van Johnson starred as Lawson.

Lawson died at his home in Chico, California, on January 19, 1992. He is interred at the Chico Cemetery Mausoleum.

Shortly after midnight, Bill Farrow, pilot of **Bat Out of Hell,** and his crew bailed out near Japanese occupied Nanchang, China. Captured by Japanese troops early the next morning, the men were thrown in prison and sentenced to death for war crimes in a mock trial. In the early hours of October 15, 1942, Farrow, Hallmark, and Spatz were taken to a nearby Chinese cemetery, blindfolded, and executed by a firing squad. Their cremated bodies were bottled and left in a crematory where they were discovered after the war. All three men are buried in Arlington National Cemetery.

A native of Darlington, South Carolina, the 24- year old Farrow was permitted to write a letter to his mother, leaving these poignant words: "Don't let this get you down. Just remember God will make everything right and that I'll see you again in the hereafter." For his service, Farrow was posthumously awarded the Distinguished Flying Cross, Chinese Order of the Clouds, Purple Heart, and Presidential Citation. In 1982 a street was named after him at the Myrtle Beach, South Carolina Air Force Base.

Sergeant Jacob DeShazer survived years in a Japanese prison camp and became a missionary to Japan after the war.
U.S. Army Photo.

Perhaps the most amazing story of all to emerge out of the daring raid is that of Staff Sergeant Jacob (Jake) DeShazer, bombardier of **Bat Out of Hell.** DeShazer spent 34 out of 40 months imprisonment in solitary confinement. Incredibly, a Japanese guard developed an admiration for the downed airman and loaned him a Bible. Through intensive study and prayer, DeShazer, the son of a Free Methodist minister, surrendered himself to God's will through Christian conversion. Despite often undergoing severe beatings by other guards, he came to accept them as fellow human beings, who needed salvation through Christ. This serene attitude enabled him to hold steady despite his dire situation. Eventually the greatest miracle of call came when Emperor Hirohito showed some unexpected mercy and commuted DeShazer's death sentence to life imprisonment.

Rescued by American soldiers on August 20, 1945, DeShazer wasted no time enrolling in Seattle Pacific College to prepare for full-time missionary service. Accompanied by his wife Florence, he returned to Japan in 1948 as a missionary under the auspices of the Free Methodist Church. He would spend the next 30 years in the land of his former enemy.

But the story does not quite end there. In 1949 DeShazer met Captain Mitsuo Fuchida, the Japanese pilot who led the fateful air strike on Pearl Harbor. The two men quickly bonded with each other. Hard times had fallen on Fuchida, and DeShazer's personal witness to a spiritual conversion offered him a hope that life, through Christ, would provide him personal peace and happiness. Under DeShazer's prodding, Fuchida converted to Christianity and devoted the rest of his life to missionary service. In 1952 he toured the United States as a member of the Worldwide Christian Missionary Army of Sky Pilots.

DeShazer lived a long and useful life, dying in Salem, Oregon, on March 15, 2008, at the age of 95.

And what else happened as a result of the Doolittle Raid? For one thing Admiral Isoroko Yamamoto, who masterminded the assault on Pearl Harbor, envisioned making another bold, perhaps knock-out, strike, against the United States, this time at the small island of Midway. By wiping out America's Pacific Fleet, he reasoned (perhaps rightly), that Japan ultimately would prevail in the war.

Beyond question, Doolittle's Raid had convinced Yamamoto that Japan was obviously vulnerable to future attacks by land based bombers. Wasting no time, he paid a personal call on Emperor Hirohito, offered his apologies, and briefly laid out his "Midway Operation" plan. The emperor liked what he saw and heard. Yamamoto could proceed full speed ahead to make Midway the next jewel in the Empire's crown.

There was only one hitch which both men failed to see. By rushing headlong into action, Yamamoto would find a rude awakening awaiting him when he again directly engaged the Americans. That subject will be covered in the next chapter.

Chapter II

Midway: *Ambush*

The epic Battle of Midway, June 4-6, 1942, is regarded as America's greatest naval victory. It is too big, too great, and too dramatic to be adequately covered in one chapter. Suffice it to say Midway was to the war in the Pacific what D-Day was to the war in Europe almost two years to the day. Perhaps more importantly, the favorable outcome to us at Midway raises the nagging question: would there have been a Normandy had we lost at Midway? The reader is advised to ponder these questions.

Ensign George Gay had never before been caught in this kind of pickle. Here he was on June 4, 1942, flying into the teeth of a Japanese strike force only hours after he lifted off the flight deck of the carrier *Hornet* as a member of Torpedo Squadron Eight.

A graduate of Texas Agricultural and Mechanical College (now Texas A&M University), Gay had joined the U.S. Navy shortly after Pearl Harbor. Hoping to see combat as a pilot, he had not expected anything like this on his first mission. All around him his buddies were falling from the skies as 35 Japanese **Zeros** struck them from every direction. Flying at only 200 miles per hour, the TBD **Devastators** were hardly a match for the much faster enemy planes.

Gay recalled the last message given by squadron commander, John C. Waldron: "If there is only one plane left to make a final run-in. I want that man to go in and get a hit. May God be with us all. Good luck, happy landing, and give 'em hell." Moments earlier Gay had last seen his skipper trying to bail out of his stricken airplane just before it exploded.

Admiral Chester Nimitz (foreground) had a surprise in store for the Japanese at Midway. Also shown Admiral Raymond Spruance, Admiral Ernest King, and Major-General Sandeford Jarman. U.S. Navy Photo.

Gay flew on through heavy debris and thick clouds of smoke. **Zero** bullets piercing into the compartment of tail gunner Bob Huntington probably killed him instantly. Gay himself felt a sharp pain above his left elbow that fortunately turned out to be only a flesh wound. As the only squadron member still flying, it was up to him to make that final run. With his electrical system blown out, he yanked the manual mechanism to release the torpedo. The missile sped toward the Japanese carrier **Soryu**. Fulfilling Waldron's admonition, Gay had gotten off the opening shot in the epic Battle of Midway. And, as we will see, he would have a ringside seat to see the epic battle through to its final conclusion.

What brought the opposing forces to Midway

What brought Gay and the ill-fated members of Torpedo Squadron Eight to tiny Midway atoll out there in the far reaches of the Central Pacific? Connected to the Hawaiian Island chain one thousand nautical miles to the south/southeast, the coral island was the site of a United States Naval Air Station. Midway served as a protective barrier for the Continental United States.

As tensions mounted between America and Japan during 1940, the United States Navy joined with private industry to set up a coalition of contractors on Midway, which actually consisted of two tiny islands: Sand housed the Contractors Pacific Naval Air Station and the 6th Marine Defense Battalion, while Eastern served as the Marine airbase. The construction layout included runways, a hanger, officers quarters, buildings, and a mall. Most of the work was completed by August 1, 1941. Defense of Midway was assigned to the Marines.

Though Midway was thousands of miles from Japan, that country's military hierarchy was alarmed over these developments. Midway would definitely be a sore point if the Japanese contemplated any future aggression against the United States.

No one had a more voracious appetite to take Midway than did Admiral Isodoru Yamamoto. Following his successful assault on Pearl Harbor, the strongly nationalistic admiral considered Midway as the next logical site where America's crippled Pacific Fleet could be drawn into battle and wiped out, thus forcing the United States into a negotiated peace. Despite Yamamoto's immense prestige at

home, Japan's Naval General Staff initially resisted undertaking any kind of operation against Midway, thinking it doubtful that the Japanese fleet could hold the atoll or even effectively operate aircraft from its runways. They were keenly aware that the U.S. 7th Air Force in Hawaii with its B-17 **Flying Fortress** bombers appeared quite capable of blasting Midway's exposed sites into smithereens, should the Japanese take the island.

Yamamoto's insistence that Japanese carriers could easily place Hawaii at risk was also called into question by the NGS, given the fact that the island outpost was being protected by long range patrols, early warning radar, and a heavy concentration of fighter planes and bombers. Indeed, the prospects of utilizing Midway against the Americans appeared quite dim to them. Those questions were quickly brushed aside once Doolittle's Raiders placed the

Fleet Admiral Isiroku Yamamoto thought by capturing Midway he could force the United States into a negotiated peace. He would find out otherwise.

Emperor's life in jeopardy by bombing Tokyo and several other Japanese cities in April. Shocked by the dramatic raid, few planners questioned the wisdom of finding a way to drive those pesky Americans away from Japanese shores and back across the Pacific.

Yamamoto's strategy was quite simple: take Midway and convert it into a base that would serve as a springboard to another powerful assault on Hawaii. Once that was done, he expected Admiral Chester Nimitz, who had succeeded Admiral Husband Kimmel as Commander of the Pacific Fleet, to react by deploying his carriers and battleships up to Midway. If all went well, the Americans would be overwhelmed by Yamamoto's powerful naval force.

To carry out this operation, Yamamoto assembled 165 ships, including four carriers, two light carriers, and seven battleships, dispersing them in several directions as he sped across the Pacific in an effort to confuse Nimitz. One portion of the armada created a feint by heading up to the Aleutian Islands, though by doing so the admiral significantly reduced the size of his Midway strike force. None of this bothered the cocky Yamamoto, who seriously doubted Nimitz possessed the capability to throw up an effective resistance once the big showdown got underway.

He was mistaken. By now Nimitz had a priceless treasure at his disposal: his cryptanalysts, dubbed HYPO, had effectively broken the Japanese code and were hourly tracking Yamamoto's movements.

Enter Joseph J. Rochefort, American cryptanalyst

In order to understand the conditions leading up to Midway and the forces that affected the battle's outcome, we must not overlook Joseph J. Rochefort, one of America's great unsung heroes of the war in the Pacific. Though he received little public recognition until well after the war was over, he is perhaps the one individual who was most responsible for America's notable victory at Midway. Interestingly, he did it quietly, covertly, and far removed from the battle itself.

Rochefort had enlisted in the Navy in 1918. Cryptanalytic operations (deciphering coded messages) and intelligence gathering quickly became his forte. In early 1941 he was promoted to Officer in Charge of Station HYPO in Hawaii. Fluent in speaking and deciphering Japanese, he thoroughly understood both the possibilities and limitations of developing radio interception of enemy communications. Rochefort's close friendship with Edwin T. Layton, the chief intelligence officer for Admiral Husband Kimmel, Commander of the Pacific Fleet in 1941,

turned out to be a fortuitous one. Japan's Pearl Harbor attack that critically wounded America's Pacific Fleet, resulted in Kimmel's dismissal and raised questions about the ability of HYPO itself to monitor Japan's intentions.

In 1985, however, Layton authored a blockbuster book, **AND I WAS THERE: PEARL HARBOR and MIDWAY — BREAKING THE SECRETS**. In the book he accused Washington's War Plans Division of depriving him, Rochefort, and Kimmel of critical intelligence gathering concerning Japanese plans prior to Pearl Harbor. By doing so, HYPO was left with one arm tied behind its back as it tried to interpret Japan's diplomatic cypher.

In any case, America's drubbing at Pearl Harbor deeply affected Rochefort. Determined that such a debacle would never happen again on his watch, he and his team redoubled their efforts to break into the Japanese military code, JN-25. Introduced in 1939, the code initials simply meant "Japanese Navy." Working day and night in their cramped, windowless, quarters in the basement of Pearl Harbor's 14th Naval District Administration Building, the Rochefort group had successfully interpreted most of the code by January 1942, an amazing accomplishment by any stretch of the imagination.

Shortly after the Doolittle Raid, decrypted enemy messages coming through to HYPO indicated that the Japanese were assembling a huge carrier task force, that would try to lure the America's Pacific Fleet into a major showdown, though the specific site of the attack was unclear. The target was simply designated "AF." It was anyone's guess what "AF" stood for.

Toiling away in his stuffy quarters Joe Rochefort was not fooled! To the contrary, he was convinced that "AF" meant Midway and that the Japanese attack would come on or about June 4. Often working 36 hour stints in his bathrobe, Rochefort drove himself and his men unsparingly to be absolutely sure their decoding was correct. This critical information would be forwarded to Nimitz, who would ultimately decide how and where the crippled American fleet would confront the Japanese Task Force which was then spreading out over the Central Pacific. No question about it, an extremely heavy burden rested on Rochefort's shoulders.

Midway's unsung hero, Joseph J. Rochefort, USN. He and his HYPO team cracked the Japanese code and were able to determine where the Japanese would attack in June 1942. U.S. Navy Photo.

With the aid of HYPO member Jasper Holmes, Rochefort came up with a clever ruse to bait the Japanese into tipping their hand. Word was sent out that American forces stationed on Midway were running short of fresh water. The Japanese took the bait: AF was running short of fresh water, an intercepted message said. Now convinced of the enemy's intentions beyond any shadow of a doubt, Rochefort sent his report to Layton who took it to Nimitz.

"Not so fast," said Washington's decoders who believed if an attack were to come, it would occur at Port Moresby or the Aleutians about the middle of June. Caught between two opposing points of view, Nimitz carefully assessed his limited options. He could accept the word of HYPO, his local fellows, or listen to Washington which had the support of Admiral Ernest King, his boss. Nimitz thoughtfully weighed the options given him and showed his leadership by wisely backing the Rochefort-Layton team.

By now Nimitz had no time to waste. A major battle was at hand and he must gather a fleet together. Though the United States Navy was still gravely unprepared for a major battle, Nimitz would, nevertheless, be ready this time to take the fight to the overly-ambitious enemy. An ambush lay just ahead.

While Nimitz hurriedly, but carefully, cobbled together his force, Admiral Yamamoto's gigantic flotilla was moving inexorably toward Midway. With what he considered well laid plans to nudge America's shattered Pacific Fleet out into open combat, Yamamoto expected to complete what he left undone at Pearl Harbor. Also confident of the outcome of the approaching naval battle, Japan's Imperial General Headquarters had already renamed Midway "Glorious Month of May."

With plenty of firepower at his disposal, Yamamoto had good reason to be cocky. His four heavy carriers **Soryu**, **Kaga**, **Akagi**, and **Hiryu** were among the best in the world. And, of course, there were the two light carriers, seven battleships, including Yamamoto's flagship, **Yamato**, and an assortment of cruisers, destroyers, submarines, and transports—

approximately 165 vessels in all. Crowded aboard the carriers were 73 fighter planes, 86 dive bombers, and 93 torpedo planes. They would be flown by some of Japan's top naval pilots, many of them dreaming of a spectacular follow-up to Pearl Harbor.

Given his limited time to prepare for the coming showdown, there was no way Admiral Nimitz could counter such a powerful force. The group he patched together included three carriers **Enterprise** and **Hornet,** commanded by Rear Admiral Raymond A. Spruance, and a crippled **Yorktown**, commanded by Rear Admiral Frank Fletcher), six cruisers, 15 destroyers, and 19 submarines. Compared to what the enemy would throw at him, it wasn't much but it would have to do

Lining the flight decks of the American carriers were 77 **F4F** *Wildcats*, 112 **SBD** *Dauntlesses*, and 42 **TBD** *Devastators,* one of the slowest airplanes in service. They would be flown by charged-up but largely untested pilots. On the surface it appeared that the coming Midway battle bore all the earmarks of a mismatch. Nimitz, however, knew that though the odds against him appeared quite daunting, they had been substantially reduced due to the fine work of his cryptanalysts.

Nimitz prepares for battle

Midway understandably offered Japan a tempting strategic target in its quest to control the Pacific. Capturing it would leave America's Pacific outpost at Pearl Harbor, almost 1,200 miles away, vulnerable to attack and possible capture. With virtually no fleet left to resist future Japanese encroachments, America would likely be forced into an early negotiated peace with Japan, clearly the aggressor nation.

Yamamoto came in from the northwest on virtually the same line he used leading up to his assault on Pearl Harbor. Meanwhile, Nimitz wisely had reinforced the Midway garrison with 17 long-range B-17 *Flying Fortresses,* 25 PBY *Catalinas*, and 3,000 more troops. "Can you hold this place," Nimitz queried his commanders. To a man they said they could and would.

Things quickly started unraveling for Yamamoto when he sent a large portion of his force off to the Aleutians to attack Dutch Harbor, a ruse he thought would draw Nimitz away from Midway. Nimitz, of course, did not take the bait since he was convinced Midway was Yamamoto's primary objective. Coinciding with the Aleutians foray, the Japanese Strike Force, including the four big carriers, began knocking out planes and installations on Midway. Once the tiny atoll was neutralized or overrun, as he expected, Yamamoto would then wipe out the American fleet he expected would come up from Pearl Harbor to defend it.

Naval squadrons blast Japanese Strike Force

Unfortunately for Yamamoto, his Strike Force commander, Vice-Admiral Chuichi Nagumo, operating from *Akagi*, felt uneasy about the mission and seemed to lack a "fighting spirit," as one observer noted.

Despite his misgivings, Nagumo's first wave of 108 planes struck Midway at the crack of dawn on June 4. Opposing them were 54 Marine Corps fighters and dive bombers and six navy torpedo bombers. No hits were scored on the enemy fleet by the interceptor planes. Yamamoto, however, had clearly tipped his hand. Waiting impatiently at a spot down range designated "Point Luck," the American Task Force would soon make its move at a time ideally suited to confront the Japanese armada.

Just as the planes were returning to the carriers following their early morning assault, a Japanese scout plane reported seeing enemy ships approaching Midway. What a shocker that must have been to the hesitant Nagumo! What was the American fleet doing that far north of Pearl Harbor?

Meanwhile, Navy pilots aboard *Hornet*, *Enterprise*, and *Yorktown* were scrambling into their torpedo planes and dive bombers. Flying off *Hornet* that morning, Lieutenant Commander Waldron's Torpedo Squadron 8 was the first group to make contact with the enemy, only to be easily picked off by the much faster **Zeros.** The lone survivor was Ensign Gay. Once in the water, he managed to hide himself under a seat cushion, and was able to witness the battle with a ringside seat of sorts a thousand or so yards from the battle site. He was picked up by a PBY the next day.

Enterprise's Torpedo Squadron 6, led by Lieutenant

Pilots flying off the carrier ENTERPRISE played key roles in turning the tide at Midway.

The "Big E" withstood heavy attacks throughout the war in all but her final battle. U.S. Navy Photo.

Commander Eugene E. Lindsey, arrived on the scene moments later and suffered a similar fate. Lindsey was among those lost and only four planes survived. *Yorktown's* Torpedo Squadron 3 quickly lost seven of its planes, including that of its squadron commander Lance E. Massey.

Only six of the 41 **Devastators** in the air that morning made it back to their carriers. Waldron, Lindsey, and Massey all died in what appeared to be a senseless effort against insurmountable odds. All three men were graduates of the United States Naval Academy and considered seasoned professionals. Not one torpedo made its mark. Was their sacrifice in vain?

Not by a long shot! Though initially things had gone badly for the outmanned Americans, the **Devastators** actually had done their job quite well by buying precious time, albeit at a terrible price. **Zeros** that had blown them out of the skies were now thirsty for gas and trying to refuel on the carrier decks. Exposed bombs and fuel lines made the enemy carriers quite vulnerable. The curtain was about to go up on act two of the mighty Midway drama that was unfolding on the Pacific.

In the annals of United States Naval history there is not found a gutsier pilot than Lieutenant Commander Clarence Wade McClusky. As leader of **Enterprise's** 37 dive bomber air group that morning, he arrived at the point where the Japanese fleet was expected to be but was not there. Though running low on fuel, McClusky flew on for another 10 minutes. Following his instinct he turned right and spotted an enemy destroyer and decided to trail it. Sure enough, just ahead he found the entire Japanese fleet trying to pull itself together after getting bumped by the torpedo squadrons. No fighter cover was evident and immobilized planes were strewn all over the flight decks.

In little more than a split second McClusky aligned his air group in attack formation, leveled the planes off at approximately 14,500 feet and led them down at full throttle. Cascading down at a 70 degree angle in a scene resembling an endless, rushing waterfall, they closed in on the tempting target far below. Joining them at the last moment was Lieutenant Commander Maxwell Leslie's Bombing Squadron 3 off **Yorktown**.

Taking direct hits, **Akagi**, **Kaga**, and **Soryu** exploded in loud blasts. One observer recalled that **Akagi's** flight elevator was blown into a "mass of molten metal." The flight deck erupted into an inferno that quickly enveloped planes waiting to take off or refuel. With bombs, torpedoes, and fuel storage tanks exploding all over the place hundreds of men were burned alive.

Their mission over, the ecstatic pilots headed home leaving behind them destruction and confusion on the high seas.

Nagumo initially resisted efforts by his staff to transfer his flag to a nearby cruiser, *Nagara*. Though stunned, shocked and dumbfounded, he finally stumbled over to a rope, climbed down to the bridge, then worked his way through stacks of dead bodies to a waiting boat. In the distance *Soryu* and *Kaga* were also pitching and tossing from the direct hits they had taken from 500 pound bombs. Doomed, fear-stricken men were seen running across the decks seeking safety that no longer existed. Many of them were cremated alive as the ships burned out of control. Some pilots died while sitting in their cockpits preparing to go up again.

Kaga sank three hours later and *Soryu* was gone by sunset. *Akagi*, although fatally stricken, seemed determined to go out in a blaze of glory, an exit she was denied. Four hundred miles away aboard his command ship Yamamoto ordered the doomed ship torpedoed and sent to a watery grave.

Though three big carriers were gone *Hiryu* still remained well out of the battle zone. Commanded by Rear Admiral Tamon Yamaguchi, the ship soon had 18 dive bombers in the air. One hundred miles away they found *Yorktown* and prepared to attack. *Yorktown*, however, was determined to put up a spirited fight. Fighter patrol planes hovering above the carrier either destroyed or crippled 10 incoming enemy planes, while antiaircraft fire from nearby cruisers and destroyers downed two more. Unfortunately, several planes got through the screen and blasted the ship. Within an hour and a half engineers and damage control groups got the crippled vessel up and running long enough for it to launch a few more planes, only moments before another wave of enemy torpedo bombers inflicted more damage to the embattled ship. Captain Elliott Buckmaster (Admiral Fletcher had been transferred to a cruiser) issued orders to abandon ship.

Meanwhile, a search plane notified Spruance on *Enterprise* of *Hiryu's* location, along with information about its formidable complement of battleships, cruisers, and destroyers. Brushing aside any thought of danger, Spruance launched his dive bombers and minutes later *Hiryu* took four direct hits. The hapless ship sank just as the sun was setting.

Yorktown might have survived the attack had not a Japanese submarine nailed it with another torpedo the next day. Finally succumbing to its mortal wounds, the hardy vessel, having put up a spirited fight to the end, rolled over and sank beneath the surface.

What Midway accomplished

Yamamoto reportedly received word of the loss of his four big carriers while engaged in a game of chess. Glancing up he muttered "Ah so" and resumed playing. When the game was over, he calmly ordered his small carriers to join Nagumo's force, thus signaling that he would continue to press the fight since the rest of his fleet remained virtually intact. Later he thought better of it and on June 7 began a general withdrawal back to Japan. The memorable Battle of Midway was over with America the clear victor.

All of the principal Japanese leaders who fought in the battle died ignominiously. Yamaguchi lashed himself to a pole and went down with his ship, preferring death to the ignominy of defeat. In 1943 Yamamoto was killed when his aircraft was intercepted over Bougainville by P-38's and shot down. Nagumo committed suicide in 1944.

By contrast Nimitz, Spruance, and Fletcher are gratefully remembered today. A destroyer carries Fletcher's name. He died in 1973 and is buried in Arlington National Cemetery.

Spruance went on to direct the naval campaigns in the Gilbert, Marshall, and Marianas Islands, Iwo Jima, and Okinawa. After the war he served as president of the Naval War College and ambassador to the Philippines. A class of destroyers bears his name. He died in 1969 at age 83 and is buried in California's Golden Gate National Cemetery.

Nimitz later served his country as Chief of Naval Operations. Several public schools are named after him, as well as museums, libraries, and a couple of prominent highways. In 1975 America's first nuclear powered carrier was launched, the **USS Nimitz**. He passed away in 1975 and is also buried in the Golden Gate National Cemetery.

Losses were heavy on both sides. The Japanese lost their four big carriers, one cruiser, and 332 aircraft, most of them destroyed while still on the flight decks. Approximately 3,500 men were killed in the battle. By comparison, the Americans lost one carrier, one destroyer, 98 aircraft, and 307 men to death. Beyond question these were terrible, irreplaceable loses for our country and the families back home. Still by giving up so much the men of Midway had miraculously turned the tide of battle in the Pacific in only six months since the infamous attack on Pearl Harbor. Japan would now play defense throughout the remainder of the long and costly war.

The handwriting was clearly on the wall: America had bounced back and ultimate victory was assured.

Ill-fated members of Torpedo Squadron Eight on board HORNET. Ensign George Gay (circle) was the only survivor of the group. Commander Waldron is shown third from left on the second row. U.S. Navy Photo.

Chapter III

"Butch" O'Hare: *First Hero*

Ever wonder what it was like to face down a desperado on Dodge City's main street back in the days when the "Wild West" was alive and well? If you get the picture, that's kind of the way it was during World War II, when aerial combat got very close against a sworn adversary. The outcome of such contact was quite obvious: one person would not be going home after the big shootout.

Similarly, Lieutenant Commander Edward "Butch" O'Hare reveled on pushing aerial combat to the limit. A fearless man of unquestioned heroism, he was a sky warrior who made the ultimate sacrifice for his country at a much too young age.

Born March 13, 1914, in St. Louis, Missouri, Butch was the son of Edward Joseph and Selma Anna (Lauth) O'Hare. An exceptionally astute lawyer, the elder O'Hare made his fortune by operating dog racing tracks in Chicago, Miami, and Boston. When their parents divorced in 1927, Butch and two younger sisters, Patricia and Marilyn, remained with their mother in St. Louis, while their father headed to Chicago to seek new and loftier heights as a lawyer for Al Capone, the noted boss/gangster of that era.

However, during Capone's tax evasion trial in 1931, the elder O'Hare, known as "Easy" Eddie, turned over incriminating evidence against Capone to

With movie star looks, Butch O'Hare was clearly America's first hero of World War II. U.S. Navy Photo.

Frank J. Wilson, the Federal investigator with the Internal Revenue Service. His cooperation with the government proved critical in putting the mob leader away for 11 years in Alcatraz Prison. Payback time came to O'Hare, however, on November 9, 1939, when he was gunned down in his car by Capone henchmen on the outskirts of downtown Chicago.

Despite his shady lifestyle, Eddie O'Hare was deeply devoted to Butch and tried to pass along to his son his own fascination with guns and flying. A stickler for discipline, he sent the 13 year old youngster off to the Western Military Academy in Afton, Illinois, where Butch excelled as a student and became an excellent marksman. In the class behind him was another bright young fellow by the name of Paul Tibbets, who one day would pilot the B-29 that dropped the atomic bomb on Hiroshima.

In 1933 Butch headed to the United States Naval Academy at Annapolis, Maryland. Since Butch's acceptance by the Academy closely coincided with his father's crucial role in obtaining Capone's conviction, some people have speculated that he did so to ensure Butch's future career as a naval pilot.

Though that possibility has never been definitively established, it is interesting to note that Butch got his appointment through the office of St. Louis Congressman John J. Cochran, one of Eddie's close friends. Graduating with the rank of Ensign on June 3, 1937, Butch was required to serve two years on surface ships before he could start his flight training at Pensacola Naval Air Station in1939.

After completing his aviation training in May 1940, Butch was assigned to the *USS Saratoga's* Fighting Three Squadron. There he forged an important bond with the already legendary John "Jimmy" Thach, his executive officer. A 1927 Annapolis graduate, Thach quickly noted that O'Hare was no ordinary green pilot. This fellow took to the heavens as though the sky belonged to him. Butch was Thach's kind of aviator.

Thach was also a brilliant technician who anticipated events before they happened. In July 1941 he took Fighting Three to San Diego to exchange the group's Brewster F2A-3s for the speedier Grumman F4F-3 *Wildcats*. While he was there, he discovered that

LCDR "Butch" O'Hare, second from left, shown aboard USS INDEPEDENCE, September 1943. Left to right: LTJG Alex Vraciu (O'Hare's wingman), LT Sy Mendenhall, and LTJG Willie Callan. Courtesy Alex Vraciu

Japan's new carrier based fighter, the Mitsubishi A6M2, touted impressive maneuverability, climb rate, and speeds reaching 380 mph. Aware that America's line of fighters were no match for such an awesome flying machine should war break out between the two countries, Thach decided on his own to come up with a plan that would defuse the **Zero's** obvious aerial advantages.

In our sophisticated age of professional thinkers and planners, what Thach accomplished by simply spreading out a bunch of matchsticks on his kitchen table completely boggles the mind. Growing up in Pine Bluff, Arkansas, Thach kept things as simple as possible when attacking a difficult problem. Over the course of several nights, he spread the matches out on the table while he tried to develop a new formation which would effectively counter the **Zero's** maneuverability edge. Too, he must come up with a way by which the **Wildcats** could hold onto a defensive position long enough to get in some shots. Flying in the traditional tight formation of six or four planes was obviously an obsolete arrangement when going up against the speedier **Zeros.**

He found his answer by arranging the several sections abreast of each other at a distance that represented the turning radius of the aircraft, thus providing the opposing sections a clear view of each other. If one wing were attacked, then the other fighters could readily come to the rescue. Once the enemy fighters took the bait and were sucked into the hook's web, as it were, there was little chance they could escape despite their edge in maneuverability.

Dubbed the "Beam Defense Position," the tactic was later renamed the "Thach Weave," the term by which it is still known today. To test his scheme, Thach tapped Butch to lead four **Wildcats** in a series of simulated attacks against his (Thach's) three F4F defenders. Each time Thach's fighters either ruined O'Hare's attack, or effectively maneuvered themselves into an advantageous position to fire back. Unfortunately, the top naval brass failed to see the new foil's possibilities and it was not used until the Battle of Midway, June 4-6, 1942.

Following the Japanese attack on Pearl Harbor, the carrier **U.S.S. Lexington** with Fighting Three aboard in early 1942 was sent to the South Pacific to strike the huge Japanese naval-air base at Rabaul, New Britain. Unfortunately, the **Lexington** was spotted 400 miles away on February 20 by a Japanese patrol plane. Thach himself shot down the intruder but not before it had radioed the carrier's position. Later that day he led six **Wildcats** against nine enemy **Betty** bombers, shooting down one and damaging two more.

Butch takes charge of sky; saves Lexington

But the danger to the carrier quickly grew. When more Japanese bombers were tracked by the carrier's radar, **Lexington** sent up six **Wildcats**, led by Thach, to meet them head-on. With not a moment to spare, O'Hare and his wingman, Marion "Duff" Dufilho, spotted nine bombers just as they appeared on the distant horizon making a beeline for the carrier. Flying some 1500 feet above the oncoming attackers, they would stand alone since the other planes were too far away to help out.

Here were two American pilots in their first dogfight facing odds considerably greater than those dealt to Gary Cooper in the blockbuster movie "High Noon." In that cinematic shootout, the town marshal was pitted against "only" four desperadoes. By contrast, the odds against the Americans grew even worse when Dufilho's guns jammed and he was forced to drop out of the fight. Now it was only Butch who stood between the virtually defenseless **Lexington** and the enemy bombers fast approaching in their vaunted V formation. Another split second might well seal the fate of 2,000 men in the ship down below. Butch O'Hare was facing "High Noon" over the Pacific.

Despite the danger and the heavy odds against him, Butch unhesitatingly shot his **Wildcat** forward in a high-side diving attack utilizing deflection firing, and headed directly into the cluster of enemy planes. A fiery machine-gun blast eliminated the last two planes on the right side of the V. On his next pass he disposed of another bomber that trailed behind on the left side of the formation. Coming in from the port side on his third run, O'Hare blew the enemy squadron leader out of the skies. One final pass and plane number five tasted a similar fate. Armed with four 50 caliber guns and 450 rounds per gun, O'Hare had used his resources wisely. Five planes were gone and his ammunition exhausted.

At that critical moment the other *Wildcats* arrived to finish off the remaining Bettys. Thach reported seeing three bombers falling simultaneously in flames as a result of O'Hare's heady action.

Barrett Tillman, in his book **The Wildcat During World War II**, noted: "It is said that twentieth century wars are decided by weight of what strategists like to call fire superiority. The lone man, the solitary marksman, is considered a relic of the past, for presumably he can make no difference in modern warfare. But the fate of one-third of the Pacific Fleet's carrier strength now depended solely upon just such a man."

It was an amazing aerial feat by any standard, carried out by a man who was ideally suited for just such a moment. With his movie star looks, moral courage, and heroic action, Butch O'Hare soon became America's first authentic hero of World War II.

Butch becomes America's national hero

Promoted to the rank of Lieutenant Commander, Butch and his wife Rita, whom he had married in September, 1941, were invited to the White House, where, on April 21, 1942, President Roosevelt personally awarded him the Medal of Honor, making him the first Navy pilot to receive the honor. The Citation read in part:

Lt. O'Hare, by his gallant and courageous action, his extremely skillful marksmanship in making the most of every shot of his limited amount of ammunition, shot down 5 enemy bombers and severely damaged a sixth before they reached the bomb release point. As a result of his gallant action–one of the most daring, if not the most daring, single action of the history of combat aviation–he undoubtedly saved his carrier from serious damage.

On April 25, 60,000 people turned out in St. Louis to honor their hometown hero with a festive noon parade, that featured Butch seated between Rita and his mother in the backseat of a black open Phaeton Packard. Included in the gala event was the military band from Jefferson Barracks, marching veterans, and a six man Marine honor guard that strode alongside the car.

Butch succeeded Thach as commander of VF-3 two

months later and went to Maui, Hawaii, where he was in charge of training other pilots in combat tactics. Still yearning to get back into action, he got his opportunity in August, 1943, when he was assigned to the light carrier *USS Independence* and sent to the recently occupied Gilbert Islands. Upon arriving there, he transferred over to the celebrated *USS Enterprise* as Air Group Commander. Now equipped with the new F6F Grumman *Hellcat,* America's fighter pilots in the Pacific owned the skies.

Standing proudly in front of his HELLCAT fighter; a smiling "Butch" O'hare poses with Chief Williams aboard the INDEPENDENCE. Courtesy Alex Vraciu.

In an effort to counter their loss of air supremacy, the Japanese, operating from their bases in the nearby Marianas Islands, came up with a clever scheme of sending torpedo-armed Bettys on regular low-level night missions against the American carriers. Rear Admiral Arthur W. Radford, commander of the Northern Carrier Group, instructed Butch to put together a plan by which the carriers could more effectively protect themselves against the costly air strikes.

The plan Butch produced included using two *Hellcats* and one TBF *Avenger*. Though large and slow, the *Avenger* provided enough room to carry the primitive and bulky radar devices in use at that time. By utilizing this method, *Enterprise's* Fighter Director Officer (FDO), who had the job of spotting incoming flights, could notify the *Avenger* of the approximate position of the enemy planes. The information would then be radioed from the *Avenger* to the **Hellcats** who would intercept and shoot down the planes.

The plan got its first test on the night of November 27, 1943. Earlier in the day the FDO picked up an inbound group of twenty Bettys. Butch and his wingman, Andy Skon, hopped aboard two "Cats," while Lieutenant Commander Phil Phillips took the controls of the **Avenger**. Alvin Kernan was Phillips's rear gunner. Somehow the system went amok and the "Cats" got separated from the **Avenger**, just as the Japanese planes came in at wave top level and began attacking the outer screen of ships protecting the carriers. Moments later Phillips, O'Hare, and Skon finally linked up.

Approaching the **Avenger** from the rear, Butch told Phillips to turn on the white, bright light directly behind the pilot's headrest. "Hey Phil," he radioed, "turn those lights on. I want to be sure it's a yellow devil I'm drilling." Butch turned on his lights, too, thus enabling Kernan to see him slide in behind the **Avenger** on the right with Skon to the left. At almost the same moment, Kernan spotted a Japanese plane suddenly appear from nowhere behind and slightly above Butch. He shouted: "Lookout Butch, there's a Jap on your tail." The urgent warning came a split-second too late. The bomber opened fire and Butch's plane vanished into the darkness.

And so Butch O'Hare, the one man who had stood between life and death at a crucial point in the early days of World War II, vanished forever into history. Though his body was never recovered, Butch was

Lt. Cdr: John S. Thach, Commanding Officer of Fighting Squadron 3. U.S. Navy Photo

given a solemn pontifical Mass in the St. Louis Cathedral on December 20, 1943. Mourning his loss, Admiral Radford remembered the gallant pilot as being "universally liked." His former classmate Paul Tibbets recalled Butch as a "hell of a fine man."

Would Butch O'Hare be forgotten as have so many extraordinary young men who asked little and gave much to turn the tide of battle against a relentless foe?

Perhaps not! On April 4, 1947, Colonel Robert R. McCormick, publisher of the Chicago *Tribune,* proposed renaming a small airport on the outskirts of Chicago. Today airline passengers boarding or passing through Chicago's massive O'Hare International Airport's Terminal Two, frequently pass a memorial to one Lieutenant Commander Edward "Butch" O'Hare. If they take time to pause and peruse the words on the plaque, they will find that the giant facility is an enduring reminder of an incredible man who, incidentally, never lived in Chicago.

Handsome "Butch" O'Hare left a rich legacy. Chicago's O'Hare Field bears his name.

Chapter IV

Four Chaplains: *Greater Love*

Very likely most readers of this book are acquainted with the familiar, albeit simple Bible verse found in John 15:13: "Greater love hath no man than this, that a man lay down his life for his friends." That verse is illustrated no better than to note the lives of four World War II chaplains, who made the ultimate sacrifice **together** to save several young soldiers as a stricken ship sank beneath the icy waters of the North Atlantic.

This heroic, tragic tale of personal sacrifice above self began on January 23, 1943, when the USAT (US Army Transport) **Dorchester**, a 5,649 ton troopship, lifted anchor in New York. The old vessel had known better days. Built in 1926, **Dorchester** once had ridden the waves of the Atlantic Ocean as a handsome luxury liner, but now was regarded by many seamen as little more than a hollow shell of what she was in her glory days.

Trudging up the long gangplank that day were 751 mostly frightened, young soldiers, most of them only teenagers and recent draftees. The trip would take these ill-prepared youngsters through Greenland on their way to face their first combat on bloody European battlefields. Counting the crew and some civilian workers, the ship was packed to the limit with 904 passengers. At St. John's, Newfoundland, **Dorchester** joined convoy S.G.-19, consisting of two merchant ships, **Lutz** and **Biscaya**, along with three Coast Guard cutters: **Comanche, Escanaba**, and **Tampa**. This small complement of ships was given the unenviable task of getting **Dorchester** safely through a highly dangerous corridor in the North Atlantic, dubbed "Torpedo Alley," a term given that part of the ocean because of the heavy presence of German U-Boats and enemy mines placed there to impede the transportation of reinforcements to the European Theatre.

Also going aboard that day with the young soldiers were four Army chaplains. Though fairly young themselves, these men were all seasoned ministers who held the rank of lieutenant. Two of the men were Protestant ministers, George L. Fox and Clark Poling; a Catholic priest, Father John Washington; and a Jewish Rabbi, Alex Goode. Each man was totally dedicated to ministering to the young soldiers placed under their spiritual care and direction. It was a big undertaking for only four men to serve the spiritual needs of such a large group, many of whom were away from home for the first time in their lives.

George L. Fox

At 42 years of age, Fox was the old timer of the group. Born on March 15, 1900 in Lewiston, Pennsylvania, he fudged on his age and ran away from home in order to join the Army during World War I. While serving on the Western Front as a medical orderly, he rescued a wounded soldier from a battlefield seething with poison gas. Later he sustained a broken back during an artillery charge. In recognition of his brave actions under fire, he was awarded the Croix de Guerre, Purple Heart, and Silver Star.

After the war, Fox completed high school and attended Moody Bible Institute in Chicago, later graduating from Illinois Wesleyan University. He spent several years in Vermont as a successful public accountant. Still, he felt his life lacked something, so he enrolled in Boston University's School of Theology to pursue studies leading to full time service in the pastoral ministry. Standing only 5 feet 7 inches tall, he was dubbed "The Little Minister" while leading several Methodist churches. His broader ministry, however, took him into hospitals and children's welfare centers in Illinois, New Hampshire, and Vermont, where he served as chaplain for the American Legion.

Following the Japanese attack on Pearl Harbor in December 1941, a deeply affected Fox, who had never forgotten his service during World War I, told his wife: "I've got to go. The boys will need me." She readily agreed. On the day he joined the army, his son, Wyatt, also enlisted in the Marine Corps. Eventually, he was admitted to Chaplains School at Harvard University.

Alexander D. Goode

Born in Brooklyn, New York, on May 10, 1911, Alexander Goode, 31, was one of four children of a Jewish rabbi who later led a Jewish congregation in Washington, D.C. A brilliant, thoughtful youngster, Goode grew up in awe of America's patriotic symbols, particularly the Declaration of Independence and the United States Constitution. His devotion to his country was clearly revealed on Armistice Day 1921, when the body of America's first Unknown Soldier was laid to rest in Arlington National Cemetery outside the Nation's Capital. Goode, then only a teenager, walked a total distance of 30 miles to and

from the ceremonies rather than take the bus. In this humble manner, he expressed his heart-felt gratitude to the men who paid the ultimate price during World War I.

Following in his father's footsteps, Goode became a rabbi. Like Fox, he found that step was not enough to satisfy his spiritual quest to help people. How, he wondered, could he bring healing to humanity without knowing how to heal their bodies? To that end, he actually completed a medical degree from John Hopkins University while continuing his rabbinical duties.

The outbreak of World War II brought Goode to another crucial point in his life. Turned down by the Navy for the chaplaincy, he was accepted into the Army in 1942 and enrolled in Harvard at the chaplain's school. After a brief assignment at an airbase in Goldsboro, North Carolina, he sought and soon received an assignment overseas.

John P. Washington

John P. Washington, 34, was one of seven children born to Irish immigrants, Frank and Mary Washington. Born on July 18, 1908, he grew up as a street savvy sort of kid who lived much of his time on the streets of Newark, New Jersey. Despite his limited economic and social background, there was a sensitive side to young Johnny's life. He loved good music, sang in the children's church choir, and became an altar boy when he was in the sixth grade. He proved to be a good athlete, and was quite intelligent and hard-working. While in high school, he felt a strong calling into the priesthood and concentrated on courses that would prepare him for that service. Following his graduation from Darlington Catholic Seminary in 1933, he met the conditions to enter the Roman Catholic priesthood in June 1935.

When America was drawn into World War II, Washington initially wanted to lay aside his clerical garb and serve on the front lines for his country. He actually did a few weeks of basic training at Fort Benjamin Harrison outside Indianapolis, Indiana, but soon transferred into the chaplaincy and enrolled at Harvard.

Clark V. Poling

Finally, there was Clark V. Poling, 32, who was born in Columbus, Ohio, on August 7, 1910. His father Daniel A. Poling was a well known Baptist minister who had served as a chaplain during World War I. Perhaps his Dad's war stories deeply affected the son, whose sensitive temperament inclined him toward pacifism until the Japanese attack on Pearl Harbor. In the meantime, the family had relocated in Auburndale, Massachusetts, then to Poughkeepsie, New York, where young Poling developed into a star high school athlete. Though following his father into the ministry, Poling eventually united with the Reformed Church in America.

Poling graduated from Rutgers University and Yale

Divinity School. His first pastoral assignment was at the First Reformed Church in Schenectady, New York. That's where he was when World War II broke out. Setting aside his pacifist beliefs, he, like the other men, wasted no time signing up to serve as an Army chaplain — again following in his Dad's footsteps. Upon completing his work in Harvard's chaplains school, he served for a while with a transport regiment in Mississippi.

Once their preparation was completed at Harvard, the four men were assigned to Camp Myles Standish in Taunton, Massachusetts, to prepare for their overseas assignment. There they formed strong emotional bonds of friendship and brotherhood. Named after Captain Myles Standish, who had led the Pilgrims to the New World on the *Mayflower* in 1620, the camp, due to the rapid wartime buildup, had been hastily constructed in 1942 to serve as both a prisoner of war camp and departure area for troops being rushed to European battlefields. The four men entered into their ministerial assignments with alacrity, knowing full well that practically all of their charges were naïve and frightened youngsters away from home and loved ones for the first time. They spent long hours with their men, guiding them, when requested, into scriptural insights and personal solace. Possessing a keen gift of humor, each chaplain also led in planning and presenting light-hearted programs each evening to give the young soldiers an outlet for their pent-up emotions.

So there they were! Four young men who had life and love ahead of them, yet quite ready and willing to serve their God and Country. As ordained ministers who had accepted leadership positions in their churches and synagogue, they could have opted to sit out the war in favor of fulfilling their unique callings to serve their local communities. Though coming from quite different backgrounds, the men shared one common interest: a strong faith that both their God and their Country needed them at this critical moment. Three of them were married with young children. Two of them served local churches, one a parish, and the other a synagogue. All of them maintained an abiding faith that God works in the lives of people regardless of the circumstances. Soon they would be called upon to prove the truth, and, indeed, the faith that they had preached and taught to their congregations.

German sub torpedoes *Dorchester*

Commanded by Captain Hans J. Danielsen, *Dorchester* and her small convoy departed St. John's on February 1 and headed for an Army command base in Narsarsuaq in southern Greenland, and an inevitable date with destiny. Rough seas caused by a severe winter storm caused the ship to dip and sway as she plowed ahead through the winter darkness, leaving no doubt that this leg of her Atlantic voyage would be a treacherous one at that time of the year.

USS (USAT) Dorchester

Despite these adverse conditions, the four chaplains quickly proved they were quite up to the formidable task of coping with the difficult conditions existing aboard ship. As they had done at Camp Myles Standish, they mixed freely with the men; helped arrange entertainment activities to relieve the stress; and performed regular religious services. One survivor recalled that the chaplains acted like parents to the men.

To reach Greenland, it was necessary for the convoy to carefully negotiate through waters infested with U-Boats, whose lethal projectiles had already sunk numerous Allied ships. On the evening of February 2, *Tampa's* sonar detected the presence of a nearby German submarine and blinked this ominous warning to the other ships: "We are being followed." An urgent request sent to St. John's to provide anti-submarine patrol planes was denied because all of the planes were on patrol and not available. Though hoping to get through the dangerous corridor and

reach port safely, the cautionary Captain Danielsen ordered the men to sleep in their clothing and wear life jackets. Unfortunately, many men below deck disregarded the order because they found the jackets too uncomfortable in the cramped quarters.

Had they realized the wiles of the formidable adversary lying in wait for them, many of the men very likely would have taken Danielsen's order more seriously. The demon of the deep was German *U-Boat 223*, a VII-C Class German submarine constructed in Kiel, the home of a major shipyard in northern Germany along the Baltic Sea. The shipyard was especially noted for its construction of submarines. Launched in early 1942, *U-223*, equipped with five 533 mm torpedo launchers, had been on the prowl for several weeks in "Torpedo Alley" looking for prey and laying mines.

Moving inexorably along despite wracked by the blinding storm, Convoy S.G.-19 was still 150 miles from its destination when all hell broke out across the dark waters of the North Atlantic. After tracking *Dorchester* for several hours, *U-Boat 223*, captained by a tough-minded 26 year old German Submarine Commander, Karl-Jurg Wachter, finally got the doomed ship directly in its crosshairs shortly after midnight on February 3. Several deadly torpedoes unleashed at the unsuspecting vessel at approximately 1 a.m., struck the *Dorchester's* starboard side near the boiler room and well below the water line. Scores of men were killed instantly by the powerful impact, while others were trapped below deck. With power and radio contact knocked out and the ship filling rapidly with water, Danielsen ordered the crew to abandon ship.

The fatally stricken old vessel began to list to her starboard side, followed by a sharp descent by the bow into the ocean's frigid waters. Bedlam exploded above deck and down below as bewildered, critically injured men struggled to survive against overwhelming odds. As though the terrible calamity were not enough, the situation was further compounded because security precautions prevented the use of flares. Thus the fate of hundreds of innocent men was effectively sealed, as though their caskets had been prepared for them then clamped tightly shut.

During the panic-stricken moments left to the men to escape from certain death, several over-crowded lifeboats capsized. Others were unable to launch from the port side because of the ship's heavy list there. In fact, only two lifeboats out of 14 on board ship were successfully launched. Once they reached the water, men who were good swimmers found themselves in the clutches of an ocean rife with extreme hypothermia and air temperature. Trapped in such intolerable conditions, they soon gave up. By the next morning hundreds of dead bodies could be seen bobbing up and down across the unforgiving waters, kept afloat by their useless life jackets. The extreme icy waters also prevented survivors who were floundering in the water from grasping the cargo nets attached to the rescue vessels.

Though any rescue of the men appeared hopeless, if not impossible, heroic acts performed that night produced small miracles. Swimmers from *Escanaba*, clad in an early form of a wetsuit, leaped into the water carrying a long line with them. By attaching the line to many of the exhausted men, they were able to haul them safely to their ship. *Escanaba* was credited with saving 133 men from certain death, while *Comanche* pulled 97 men on board.

Chaplains lose their lives to save men

Meanwhile, despite the widespread confusion sweeping across the deck of the rapidly sinking ship, the four chaplains appeared on the scene to offer assistance and try to calm down, instill courage, and even offer hope to the frightened soldiers. Prying open a storage locker, they started distributing life jackets to the men. Just as the locker's supply was exhausted, one bewildered youngster stepped up and moaned: "Padre, I've lost my life jacket and I can't swim!" Without hesitating, the chaplain (whose identity is not known) removed his own jacket, attached it around the soldier, and said: "I won't need it." The other chaplains quickly followed suit to assist other men, thus sealing their own fate. PFC John Ladd, an eyewitness who survived the ordeal, remarked later that it was the finest thing he ever expected to see "this side of heaven."

As the lifeboats slowly drifted away from the doomed ship, the chaplains were seen silhouetted in a pale glow from a few flares, with some soldiers gathered around them in a prayerful mode, as *Dorchester* took her final gasp before going under. Standing alongside a rail, the chaplains locked their arms together and embraced each other as if to say: "We are not abandoning ship." Survivor Grady Clarke got a glimpse of this touching scene in time to see the ship's bow come up, then quickly take the doomed men to their final resting place beneath the wild waters.

Within only 23 minutes *Dorchester* was gone, and in her wake went 675 men, most of them in the flower of their youth. There were only 227 survivors. The catastrophe constituted the third largest loss of life on an American vessel on the high seas during World War II. It is not known what became of the four recipients of the four chaplains unselfish actions.

There is an interesting footnote to this tragic story. On March 30, 1944, two British destroyers, HMS *Laforey* and HMS *Tumult,* detected the presence of a submarine operating north of Palermo, Italy, in the Mediterranean. Confident that this was an enemy vessel, the destroyers dropped powerful depth charges that easily struck their mark, sending their adversary to a watery grave. U-223 had finally met the same fate she administered to *Dorchester*.

What did the chaplains give up when they surrendered their life jackets to share that greater love with the young soldiers under their care? George Fox left a wife and two children; Alexander Goode, a wife and daughter; Clark V. Poling, a wife and two children; and John P. Washington, eight brothers and sisters.

Many memorials and remembrances around the country recall their unselfish sacrifice to their fellowmen. On December 19, 1944, each man was posthumously awarded the Distinguished Service Cross and Purple Heart. President Harry Truman himself on February 3, 1951, dedicated a chapel in their honor at Grace Baptist Church in Philadelphia. Their extraordinary act inspired the commissioning of the Chaplain's Medal for Heroism in 1961, never to be repeated unless by an act of Congress. Stained glass windows placed at the United States Military Academy at West Point and the Chapel at Fort Snelling, Minnesota, also recall their selfless deed.

Of particular note, is the Four Chaplains three cent stamp which was issued by the United States Post Office on May 28, 1948. The stamp is unique for two reasons: (1) it was the first stamp to depict a Jew and (2) it was issued only five years after the men died.

1959 Postage Stamp Depicted Immortal Chaplains

Prior to that, it was customary not to honor deceased persons less than 10 years after their death. Designed by Louis Schwimmer, head of the Art Department for the United States Post Office in New York City, the stamp depicts the sinking of the **Dorchester** in the foreground, with head shots of the chaplains shown above the ship.

These special remembrances, worthy though they are, still pale in comparison to the laurels of glory each of these men wears throughout eternity. On that fatal day long ago, the Four Chaplains proved beyond any shadow of doubt that, indeed, there does exist in our often tortured world an extremely rare gift we simply call "Greater Love."

Chapter V

Get Yamamoto: *Avenge Pearl Harbor*

Mission members. Standing left to right: Roger Ames, Lawrence Graebner, Tom Lanphier, Delton Goerke, Julius Jacobson, Eldon Stratton, Albert Long, and Everett Anglin. Kneeling: William E. Smith, Doug Canning, Besby Holmes, Rex Barber, John Mitchell, Louis Kettel, and Gordon Whittakar. Not shown is Ray Hine who was lost during the mission.

Things of late had not been going well for Admiral Isoroku Yamamoto, the mastermind behind Japan's infamous attack on Pearl Harbor. As commander of the Imperial Navy's Combined Fleet, Yamamoto was recognized as his country's most capable naval strategist. His smashing of America's Pacific Fleet raised Japan's hopes to complete her Southeast Asian conquests and stretch her dreams of empire almost to America's western shores.

Indeed, during the first six months of the Pacific War, Japanese military forces appeared unbeatable as they swept victoriously throughout Southeast Asia and the Solomon Islands. Unless they could be stopped, Australia and New Zealand might well suffer a similar fate.

Fortunately, U.S. Navy Intelligence (code-named "Magic") had effectively broken the Japanese code. Armed with critical information about Japan's ambitious military intentions, America's wounded Pacific Fleet pulled itself together in time to win the crucial Battle of Midway, June 4-7, 1942. This incredible triumph over Yamamoto's powerful naval force was quickly followed up with big wins at Guadalcanal in the Solomon Islands and the Battle of the Bismarck Sea.

Having lost four carriers, one heavy cruiser, and many of his top pilots at Midway, Yamamoto now found himself in the unfamiliar position of playing defense as he plotted his next moves in the Pacific from his comfortable quarters (once the plush home of the island's governor) at Rabaul, Japan's military base on New Britain. To make matters worse, his Midway loss severely limited his ability to mount much of an attack on strategic places like Fiji, New Caledonia, Samoa, or New Guinea. America had shown she could take a punch below the belt and strike back—hard!

So, in an effort to boost sagging Japanese military morale following these critical reversals, Yamamoto in April 1943 decided that he would personally inspect some of his forward bases in the South Pacific. Bougainville would be his first stop. Little did he suspect that "Magic" on April 14 had intercepted and carefully decrypted his entire schedule for the upcoming trip.

"Magic," in fact, knew all of the specific details of his arrival and departure times, the sites he would visit, and the number and types of aircraft that would transport and cover him during his one day trip. Two medium Betty bombers would fly him from Rabaul to Ballale Airfield, which was located on an island near Bougainville, with Six Mitsubishi **Zeros** providing him protective escort. There was one hitch of which Yamamoto was completely unaware: he was well known for his punctuality in keeping appointments. Armed with this information, America this time would be quite ready to welcome him with a big surprise, not unlike the one he sprang on us at Pearl Harbor.

Clearly, the United States Navy had in its possession extremely valuable information that gave it a golden opportunity to permanently remove Yamamoto from the scene, and thus, hopefully, shorten the war. Consequently, an ambitious and highly dangerous plan was quickly put together to intercept and shoot him down during his hop over to Bougainville.

Details of Yamamoto's trip and the plan to take him down were rushed to Secretary of the Navy Frank Knox in Washington. After conferring with General Henry H. "Hap" Arnold, commander of the U.S. Army Air Corps, Charles A. Lindbergh, Frank Meyer, the chief engineer at Lockheed, and, reportedly, President Roosevelt himself, Secretary Knox gave a hearty thumbs up to the plan.

To the Navy's dismay, however, the principal participants in the mission would come from the Army Air Corps, whose pilots on Guadalcanal flew Lockheed's sleek new P-38 *Lightning* the only airplane built to carry enough fuel to intercept Yamamoto and return to base.

Major John Mitchell, who had recently assumed command of the 339th Fighter Squadron stationed on Guadalcanal, was tapped to lead the daring mission. A 28-year old Mississippian, Mitchell was plenty savvy and knew his way around. A brainy, analytical sort of fellow, he was valedictorian of his high school graduating class and attended Columbia University on a scholarship. Already a three year veteran of the Army Air Corps, his crack squadron was especially trained to fly the P-38. If any group could do the job, these were the guys.

In October 1942, Mitchell and several pilots from the 70th Fighter Squadron (his former squadron) arrived on Guadalcanal, where their training continued despite persistent harassment by die-hard Japanese soldiers who were still hidden in the bush. Henderson Field, a small strip of land carved out of the jungle, served as their make-shift headquarters. A warrior by nature, Mitchell did more than just train to fight: he utilized some of his extra time to shoot down three Japanese airplanes.

Eighteen *Lightnings* arrived on Guadalcanal shortly after the first of the year. Boasting a top speed of 395 miles per hour, this amazing twin-engine fighter exceeded any pilot's imagination. Its devastating firepower spewed out from four .50 caliber machine guns and a 20mm cannon mounted on the plane's nose. The airplane's ability to soar up to 25,000 feet in a matter of seconds kept it well out of reach of most intercepting enemy airplanes. No wonder most of the pilots loved what they considered a futuristic aircraft.

Meanwhile, back in December, several more of Mitchell's top pilots in the 70th Fighter Squadron had joined him. They included Captain Tom Lanphier, and Lieutenants Rex Barber and Doug Canning. Lanphier and Barber were regarded as among the best pilots in the Pacific at that time. Both men had five enemy kills to their credit, qualifying them as official air aces.

On April 17 Mitchell, accompanied by Lanphier, was ordered to an underground bunker at Henderson Field, two miles away from the 339th's headquarters, to meet with Admiral Marc Mitscher and other top naval brass. Entering the crowded, smoke-filled room, the two men were shown a document marked **TOP SECRET**. They could hardly believe their eyes, for here before them was the precise outline of Yamamoto's inspection trip scheduled for the next day. The following order was signed by non-other than Navy Secretary Knox:

SQUADRON 339 P-38 MUST AT ALL COSTS REACH AND DESTROY.

PRESIDENT ATTACHES EXTREME IMPORTANCE TO MISSION.

Admiral Marc Mitscher, commander of air operations in the Solomon Islands, tapped Mitchell and Lanphier to work out the specific details during the night of the proposed intercept mission. Joined by two intelligence officers, Lieutenant Joseph E. McGuigan of the Navy and Captain William Morrison of the Army, Mitchell set himself up in the mess tent, laid out maps of the Solomon Islands, and began to pour over them by lamp light. Starting with the fact that Yamamoto rarely, if ever, ran late for an appointment, Mitchell estimated a Betty bomber's speed at approximately 80 mph, or three miles per minute. If correct, this would place the intercept point over Bougainville at approximately 45 miles, or 15 minutes from the admiral's landing site at Ballale Airfield.

Calculating the total distance from Guadalcanal to the anticipated intercept point at 436 miles, Mitchell planned to fly his squadron at 198 mph approximately 50 feet above the ocean's white topped waves. The entire flight would be entirely over water to the south and west of the Solomon Islands. Though this approach meant a highly stressful mission, Mitchell believed staying close to the water offered the least possibility of detection by Japanese radar and

John Mitchell planned and led the successful mission of 16 fighters that intercepted and shot down the bomber that carried Admiral Yamamoto.

coast watchers. Meeting with the men who would comprise the mission, he solemnly warned that the odds against successfully carrying out the assignment probably stood at 1000 to one. Not one man flinched at the news. The fellows who were selected were completely reliable, totally fearless men who reveled in their role as sky warriors. Nor were they novices at their trade. To the contrary, most of them were among the top American airmen in the Pacific at that time.

Four *Lightnings* led by Lanphier were dubbed the "Killer Flight." Their job was simply to bring down Yamamoto. Once contact was made with the enemy, the other planes were directed to soar up to 18,000 feet where they would act as cover should any of the 75 Japanese fighters stationed on nearby Kahili Island come up to engage the Americans. Involvement by any of these aircraft would greatly lessen the mission's chances for a successful shoot down. Pin point timing would ultimately determine the success or failure of the operation.

While all of this was going on, an unsuspecting Yamamoto dined with several aides and retired for the night. Up bright and early the next day, he garbed himself in a dark green field uniform in place of his accustomed white dress attire, thinking this would make him less conspicuous during the inspection trip. Otherwise he was immaculate in his black boots, a handkerchief stuffed in one pocket, and white gloves on his hands. He carried a small book of poems, and a samurai sword given to him by a deceased brother. He would travel lightly, but elegantly, on this the last day of his life.

A photographer assigned to take pictures of the admiral's departure from Rabaul was a no-show. This personal slight apparently made no difference to Yamamoto, who was more interested in keeping his daily appointments on time. Instead, he hopped into a waiting car and was driven down the hill and through a thick forest to the airfield. Members of his staff followed in cars behind him.

At the airfield, Yamamoto was greeted by a group of fellow officers who showed up to bid him farewell. Resting on the flight strip were two Betty bombers, flown over earlier from another airfield seven miles away. After the officers carried out the appropriate protocol of bowing and saluting each other, Yamamoto strode over to bomber Number 323, climbed aboard, and seated himself directly behind the pilots. His chief surgeon, a naval air force officer, and secretary sat farther back in the airplane.

Occupying the second bomber, Number 326, were Vice Admiral Matome Ugaki, Chief of Staff of the Combined Fleet, He was accompanied by the staff communications officer, a naval officer, and the fleet paymaster. The engines came to life and the two bombers sped down the runway. Once in the air, they were joined by six **Zero** fighters that soon separated into two groups of three on each flank of Yamamoto's airplane.

Almost to the second Yamamoto had departed precisely on time. It was exactly 6 a.m.

Meanwhile over on Guadalcanal, Mitchell's final morning inspection reassured him that everything was in order and ready to go. He had done his best so the rest was in the hands of God. By then, word had trickled around the base that this particular mission was big beyond any stretch of the imagination. Yamamoto, the man responsible for bringing on this war, was in the crosshairs of some of America's top fighting men. Pearl Harbor would finally be avenged.

Seated in a jeep, Admiral Mitscher gave a snappy salute to the P-38s as they roared off Henderson Field's Fighter 2 airstrip promptly at 7:25 a.m. It was Palm Sunday, April 18, exactly one year after Mitscher had witnessed a similar scene when he stood on the deck of the carrier **HORNET** and bade farewell to the Doolittle Raiders.

Unfortunately, two **Lightnings** had to drop out, one because of a flat tire on takeoff and the other one when the drop tanks failed to feed fuel to the engines. Since both planes were members of the "Killer Flight" group, it was necessary for Mitchell to quickly shift Besby Holmes and Ray Hine into the vacancies. An experienced pilot, Holmes was stationed in Hawaii when the Japanese hit Pearl Harbor. He managed to get a plane aloft to briefly engage one attacking aircraft. On the other hand, Hine, though a gung ho pilot, only had limited experience at the controls of the P-38.

Though this would be the longest fighter-intercept mission of the war, Mitchell, despite lacking time to work out the plan, had correctly calculated his arrival time at the expected intercept point. Actually, he was off by one minute. At 0934 am. Doug Canning was the first to spot Yamamoto's approaching entourage and radioed: "Bogey's! Eleven O'clock High." Sure enough, there he was—the pride of the Empire— flying about 5,000 feet above Mitchell's group in a light haze that spread out across the distant sky. Mitchell saw them too, but at the moment his squadron was indiscernible as it skimmed along only a few yards above the green waters of the Pacific.

Wasting no time, Mitchell brought his men into a tight formation, selected a course parallel to that of the approaching Japanese planes, and went into a sharp power climb. At 4,500 feet he radioed Lanphier: "O.K., Tom, he's your meat." "Roger" came the confident reply as Lanphier broke off the "Killer Flight." Mitchell and the other planes continued their sharp climb up to 18,000 feet, high enough to position themselves against enemy fighters coming up after them.

Accompanied by Rex Barber, his wing man, Lanphier locked onto the two **Bettys** at approximately their three o'clock position and approached slightly below them. Seeing the American fighters rapidly approaching, the **Betty** pilots began a rapid descent toward their landing strip at Ballale. Suddenly three **Zeros** appeared on the right side of the **Bettys**, obviously trying to get behind Lanphier and Barber.

Though momentarily taken by surprise, Lanphier aggressively broke 90 degrees to the left and shot up to meet one **Zero** head on. At the same time, Barber veered off to the right and locked onto the tail of lead bomber 323, Yamamoto's aircraft. He poured fire directly into the aircraft's right engine and fuselage until the **Betty** was smoking heavily, losing speed, and rolling off to the left. As the right wing came

Tom Lanphier Jr. claimed credit for downing Yamamoto's plane. National Archives Photo.

up, Barber, while in the process of making a hard right turn, narrowly missed colliding with the plane. He last saw it in a glide angle skimming across the jungle's tree tops. It is quite likely that Yamamoto was killed by one or more of Barber's bullets.

The heady Barber soon faced yet another challenge when the pursuing **Zeros** attempted to make a vicious assault on him. Only through his skillful piloting, a bit of luck, and the P-38's great engine power was he able to escape. Glancing back over his shoulder, he saw a plume of black smoke rising from the jungle where the **Betty** had gone down.

Spotting the second bomber flying low off the water

just as it was attacked by two other **Lightnings**, Barber finished it off and sent it crashing into the water. While all this was going on, the planes flying cover briefly engaged reacting **Zeros** without making any kills. The fierce, one-sided air battle lasted barely four minutes. Able to say "Mission Accomplished" without hesitating, Mitchell broke off contact and ordered the squadron back to Henderson Field. The battle in the sky had occurred so quickly that not one Japanese plane on Ballael was able to take to the air.

Yamamoto's crash site deep in Bougainville's jungle was located by a Japanese search party the next day. Despite his being thrown clear of the plane, the admiral's body, reportedly, was still seated upright in his seat under a tree, his white gloved hand firmly gripping the hilt of his samurai sword.

As Lanphier came in for his landing on Henderson Field, he broke the tight security policy that had been imposed on the mission and radioed: "I got Yamamoto." Almost beside himself, he crowed the same story to the ground crew that gathered around his plane, and continued yelling at the top of his voice from the rear seat of a jeep that brought him down the runway. Everybody on the field quickly caught the spirit and began celebrating and slapping each other on the back. Since no serious debriefing was ordered, several years passed before Lanphier's claim was seriously challenged.

As Lanphier told it, he shot off the wing of an escorting **Zero**, then flipped upside down and circled back toward the two bombers, spotting the lead (Yamamoto's) bomber slightly below him. Coming out of a hard right angle turn, he blasted off the **Betty's** right wing, sending it crashing into the jungle.

Early on Barber challenged Lanphier's story, for which Lanphire branded him a "damned liar." In time, however, other of the mission pilots also began to question Lanphier's claim against that of Barber. Finally, the U.S. Air Force tried to strike a middle ground and awarded "half kills" to the two pilots. The heated controversy continued throughout the lifetimes of both men and, indeed, simmers to the present day.

Eventually, however, Barber's account gained the support of many groups as being the most plausible. In 1997 the American Fighter Aces Association gave him 100 percent credit for bringing down Yamamoto. The Confederate Air Force (now Commemorative Air Force) in 1998 inducted Barber into the American Combat Airman Hall of Fame for disposing of Yamamoto alone and unassisted.

Despite the mission's resounding success, those who participated were effectively removed from further service in the Pacific for the time being. The country could not risk their capture since they knew far too much about America's successful code-breaking. Consequently, the men were returned stateside for training and reassignments. Late in the war, Mitchell would return to action and shoot down three more enemy planes over Japan while flying P-51s. During the Korean War he downed four Migs. During his 23 years of impeccable military service he received many awards, among them the Navy Cross and Army Distinguished Cross before retiring as a colonel. He died on November 15, 1995.

Tom Lanphier flew 97 combat missions during the war, later serving as director of operations of the 72ⁿᵈ Fighter Wing. He downed nine Japanese planes and damaged eight on the ground. He also sank a destroyer. His service awards included receiving the Navy Cross, Silver Star, and Distinguished Flying Cross. Retiring from active duty after the war as a lieutenant colonel, Lanphier, who had majored in journalism at Stanford University, became editor of the Idaho *Daily Statesman* and Boise *Capital News*. From 1951 to 1960, he was vice-president of the Convair Division of General Dynamics in San Diego, California. After a lengthy bout with cancer, he died on November 26, 1987, and is buried in Arlington National Cemetery. To the very end of his life he adamantly claimed full credit for downing Yamamoto.

Rex Barber later saw service in China where he shot down several more enemy aircraft, and managed to barely escape capture following being shot down himself. He was also credited with sinking a destroyer. Retiring from the service in 1961 as a full colonel, he returned to his hometown of Culver, Oregon, where he served several terms as mayor and was active in various veterans organizations. He died on July 26, 2001. His son said his father had lived a rich life and, finally, passed away when his "afterburners" finally gave out.

Besby Holmes was the last member of the "Killer Group" to pass away, his death coming at age 88 on July 23, 2006, in San Francisco. He also retired from military service as a lieutenant colonel.

Despite the controversy that swirled around who shot down Yamamoto, the daring, selfless service of each pilot who flew the epic mission still stands as one of America's brightest moments during World War II. All of the young men who went aloft that day against incredible odds, played crucial roles in helping turn the tide of battle in the Pacific War. Even at this distant date they deserve to be saluted and, most of all, remembered.

Rex Barber describes his angle at the shooting down of Yamamoto's plane.

Chapter VI

"Pappy" Boyington: *Still Taking Enemy Fire*

To be sure Medal of Honor Recipient Gregory "Pappy" Boyington was one of a kind! A daring, dashing, devil-may-care sort of fellow, he was for a while America's unchallenged hero of World War II.

So far so good, but, amazingly, in February 2006 at the University of Washington, Boyington's 1934 alma mater, a flap arose when a member of the Associated Student Senate introduced a resolution recommending the erection of a suitable memorial to honor him for his war service.

Surprisingly, this simple request ignited a vocal protest from several other student legislators, prompting one member to state that she didn't "believe a member of the Marine Corps was an example of the sort of person UW wanted to produce." Another senator

opined that the university already had too many monuments to "rich, white men," obviously unaware that Boyington's ancestry connected him to the Sioux Indians. One legislator even argued that the university should not honor any person who killed others, even in war.

Why would an authentic World War II hero nicknamed "Pappy" cause so much controversy after 60 plus years had passed? Born into a home rife with poverty on December 4, 1912, in Coeur d'Alene, Idaho, Boyington spent his childhood years in St. Maries, Idaho, a rough and tumble sort of logging town in the old Northwest. Eventually the family settled in Tacoma, Washington, where eight year old Greg met the famous aviator, Clyde "Up-side-down" Pangborn, and developed an undying love for flying.

"Pappy" Boyington and his Black Sheep Squadron in the Southwest Pacific in 1943. Courtesy "Hap" Halloran.

Shown here in this classic photo, "Pappy" exuded inner strength and heroism. U.S. Marine Photo.

As the story goes, the youngster was able to finagle a free ride out of barnstormer Pangborn who was in town for an air show.

While attending the University of Washington, Boyington was a member of the wrestling and swimming teams, R.O.T.C., and Lambda Chi Alpha. No slouch at athletics, he once held the Pacific Northwest Intercollegiate middleweight wrestling title. Graduating in 1934 with a B.S. in aeronautical engineering, he moved around for a while working part time in mining and logging camps and road construction. Finally, the Boeing Corporation hired him as a draftsman.

Still, flying remained his first love and coveted goal! Enlisting in the Marine Corps in February, 1936, he wrangled an appointment to the newly formed cadet flight program, receiving his wings at the Pensacola, Florida Naval Air Station on March 11, 1937. A hell-raising but well-liked chap among his pilot buddies, Boyington was marking time as a flight instructor in Pensacola in late summer of 1941, when he heard that Clair Chennault, the head of the American Volunteer

46

Group (AVG), was looking for seasoned pilots to aid the Republic of China in her costly war against the Japanese.

Chennault, a distant relative of Confederate General Robert E. Lee, was born in Commerce, Texas, on September 6, 1893, but grew up in Waterproof, Louisiana. Also smitten with flying, he joined the Army Air Corps in 1917 and by the early 1920s was considered one of the world's top aerobatic pilots. A visionary man who saw the possibilities of using pursuit squadrons to advance America's military interests, Chennault soon found himself pitted against his superiors who favored the bomber as a more suitable weapon of war. Outspoken and utterly fearless in stating his positions, Chennault lost the argument and was drummed out of service in 1937.

Though one door was closed another one soon opened— one that would make Chennault one of those legendary figures in World War II history. Generalissimo Chiang Kai-shek appointed Chennault his advisor and vested him with the authority to build a Chinese Air Force that was capable of taking on the increasingly aggressive Japanese.

Though the United States and Japan were theoretically at peace, it was no secret that President Roosevelt was looking for ways by which to assist China in her ongoing war with the Empire. In order to separate the United States from any perceived involvement in Japan's internal affairs, the program that was initially put together operated under the cover name, Central Aircraft Manufacturing Company (CAMCO). Later it became known as the American Volunteer Group (AVG). Through this outlet, the wily Chennault was able to bring in skilled American pilots to fly missions and train Chinese airmen. The Curtiss P-40 *Warhawk* was the aircraft selected for use by the group.

Sensing a golden opportunity to get into aerial combat action as well as make a little extra money, Boyington wasted no time signing up but with the understanding that he could resume his Marine career if the United States got involved in a war which appeared likely. Hired and given the rank of flight leader, Boyington was paid $675 a month.

While flying with the "Flying Tigers," the nickname given the unit, Boyington shot down six Japanese

General Claire Chennault at a ceremony in China during the war. U.S. Army Photo.

planes, though his detractors only credited him with four. He was a member of the pre-dawn P-40 fighter sweep over the large Japanese held airfield at Chiang Mai, Thailand, on March 24, 1942. The swarming airmen wreaked havoc with their multiple strafing runs.

Brash, out-spoken, and never one to back down, Boyington eventually proved too much for even the crusty old Chennault. He was dishonorably discharged a few weeks after the raid and returned back to the states. By that time, however, America desperately needed trained men to serve in the war effort, so Boyington was recalled to service and promoted to major in the Marine Corps.

Assigned to Marine Aircraft Group 11, First Marine Aircraft Wing, he was appointed Executive Officer of VMF 122, headquartered on Guadalcanal. Shortly after arriving there he was promoted to commanding officer of the elite Marine Fighter Squadron 14, the famous "Black Sheep Squadron." At that post, Boyington initially earned the nickname "Gramps" because at 31 years of age he was a decade or more older than most of the men who served under him. The catchy moniker was changed to "Pappy" from words in a song composed by one of his pilots. This prompted war correspondents in the Pacific to use the term "Pappy" when referring to Boyington in reports sent to their newspapers. Thus, his image was permanently sealed for all time.

On September 14, 1943, the "Black Sheep" exploded across the Pacific. Beginning on that day and continuing for 84 days, the squadron's 26 pilots destroyed or damaged 197 enemy planes. Troop transports and supply ships were also sunk and ground installations wiped out.

Not surprisingly, Pappy made sure he was in the middle of the hottest action. His natural ability to handle the Vaught F4U *Corsair* greatly enhanced his growing reputation as a sky warrior. Called the "whistling death" by the Japanese, the *Corsair* could out fight and out climb any prop driven enemy airplane it went up against. During fierce action over the Russell Islands, New Georgia, and Bougainville, Pappy shot down 14 enemy fighters in 32 days. On December 17, 1943, he personally led the first fighter sweep over Rabaul, Japan's Pacific headquarters. By the end of the month his enemy kills numbered 25.

Then fickle fate dealt him a bad hand. On the morning of January 3 Pappy led a 46 plane fighter sweep once more over Rabaul. His wingman that day was another top pilot, Captain George Ashmun. Alerted to the incoming flight, approximately 76 Japanese **Zero** fighters (nicknamed Zekes by the Americans) attempted to derail the raid. Seeing about a dozen enemy planes blocking his path, Boyington aggressively went on the attack. Almost instantaneously he bagged his 26th kill, thus tying the American record set by Eddie Rickenbacker during World War I and fellow Marine, Joe Foss. Moments later he and Ashmun disappeared in a heavy haze that covered the area.

Pappy Boyington had flown his final mission. As he and Ashmun faded from view, they were jumped by a swarm of **Zeros** at about 12,000 feet. Ashmun went down nose first, his plane completely enveloped in flames. Pappy followed close on the tail of a Japanese fighter, then was jumped when several planes came up in his rear and opened fire on him. At the time Ashmun's *Corsair* smashed into the water, Boyington was only about 300 feet above him after leveling off from his steep dive. Hit in the main gas tank, Pappy's plane also burst into flames, leaving him with the sensation of "looking into an open blast door."

Parachuting out of the plane at a much too low altitude, Boyington was badly injured when he struck the water full force. For the next 15 to 20 minutes he duck-dived as **Zekes** tried to strafe him. As soon as they headed back to Rabaul, he treaded water for a couple of hours before popping open the rubber raft dangling between his legs. He lay exhausted on the raft for several hours before being picked up by a Japanese submarine.

"Pappy" languished in the Omori Prison Camp outside Tokyo during the final 19 months of the war. Subjected to horrendously cruel treatment by his sadistic captors, he was once publicly beaten with a baseball bat in front of his fellow prisoners. Refusing to let his captors humiliate or break him, he did not mummer one word during the beating. He lost 80 pounds while imprisoned. If there was a silver lining to his imprisonment, it came through the lifetime friendships he formed with some of the other prisoners. One such person was Ray "Hap" Halloran, who had been a navigator on a B-29. Halloran, who today lives today in Menlo Park, California, looked up to Boyington as a natural leader who never permitted his dire circumstances to diminish the sparkle in his eyes." I felt I would be o.k. as long as Pappy was there," Halloran recalls.

Liberated by Marine and Naval landing forces on August 29, 1945, Boyington was welcomed home as a national hero and found that he had been promoted to lieutenant- colonel during his long imprisonment. Invited to the White House, he was presented with the Medal of Honor by President Truman. He also received the Navy Cross for his daring raid on Rabaul, and was the featured star of a Victory Bond Tour. Lauded by his fellow Americans as a national hero, he retired from the Marine Corps as full colonel on August 1, 1947.

Two golf buddies and fellow POWS, "Hap' Halloran and "Pappy" pose for the camera.
Clearly, the years had not treated "Pappy" kindly. Courtesy "Hap" Halloran.

That moment of euphoria for Pappy, unfortunately, passed much too quickly. Beset with a myriad of inner demons, he shuffled around from place to place for several years, working in department stores, traveling as a liquor salesman, and refereeing wrestling matches. His disastrous family life brought on long periods of alcoholism. In 1966 he almost died of emphysema.

In time his fighting instinct eventually kicked in to provide him some bright spots along the way. His book *BAA BAA BLACK SHEEP* became a best seller in the 1950s. In the mid-1970s, a popular television series by the same name starred the noted actor Robert Conrad. Thus restored to public consciousness, a rejuvenated Pappy once again became a familiar figure on the speaking and air show circuits. He even acquired a single seat airplane and resumed flying.

A tenacious fighter to the very end, Pappy finally flew his last mission on January 11, 1988, when he succumbed to cancer in a hospice in Fresno, California. A Marine plane flew him to Washington, D.C. where four days later he was laid to rest with full military honors in Arlington National Cemetery near the Tomb of the Unknowns. Giving the eulogy for him that day was his fellow P.O.W. friend, "Hap" Halloran, who remembered Pappy as a fellow who "always wanted to be in the thick of the action, a fearless warrior, and yet a gentle, caring and considerate person." A missing man formation of F-4 fighters stationed at nearby Andrews Air Force Base paid Pappy a well deserved final salute.

Those who understand the role played by the warrior during wartime, clearly credit Boyington as among America's best. Retired Marine Corps Colonel

Charles J. Quilter, also a pilot, once described Pappy this way: "By far the most colorful Marine aviator of any era, he was pugnacious, witty, rebellious, fun loving, a disaster as a peacetime officer, a gifted pilot in both dog fighting and gunnery, and a brilliant combat leader."

Pappy's World War II exploits are not forgotten today. In 2007 the Coeur d'Alene, Idaho, was renamed "Coeur d'Alene Airport—Pappy Boyington Field." Then there is the modern version of the "Black Sheep Squadron," a Marine detachment of six AV 8B Harrier jets attached to the USS PELELIU, an amphibious assault ship. Their shields depict a black sheep, stars, a bar, and the gull-winged Corsair. Designated "Major 'Pappy' Boyington," the lead jet is flown by Major John "Bull" Rahe, the detachment's officer in charge.

So, in a real sense Pappy is still soaring high above, this time to inspire modern Marines to hang tough just as he did long ago.

Going back to that little flap at the University of Washington, there was such a loud outcry from prominent members of the alumni association against the student government's hasty action, that the original resolution was withdrawn. A new resolution supported the erection of a suitable memorial to all five alumni of the university who received the Medal of Honor. That fund-raising project is still underway.

Should he be looking on from some distant celestial outpost, would Pappy want to share the spotlight with his fellow grads? Probably not, given the fact that he was one of a kind. Still, it might be said that during his final dog fight, Pappy pretty much had the last word against a modern foe who tried to take him down, long after he had gone up against real enemies during his heady days of placing his life on the line during World War II.

Chapter VII

Bob Palmer: *Rabaul Raid*

"Now just how did I get into this situation," mused bomber pilot Bob Palmer as he bore down on the powerful Japanese military base at Rabaul. Palmer had flown combat missions before but none quite like this one. Unrelenting anti-aircraft fire was coming up from below, while Japanese **Zeros** were flitting here and there like blood-thirsty mosquitoes. What was a rural kid from Minnesota doing in a place like this on April 9, 1944, Easter Sunday?

Often regarded as the unsung heroes of World War II, America's bomber pilots asked little more than to just do their job and return safely to base, knowing full well that another mission awaited them tomorrow, and the next day, and beyond. In their hands lay not only their own personal survival but also that of their crew. The 23 year old Palmer found out this day that Rabaul was no milk run operation. Was he up to the task?

Bob Palmer was a handsome Army Air Corps officer who flew 76 combat missions.
Courtesy Bob Palmer

At one time the capital of New Britain in the Solomon Islands, Rabaul's 1,400 Australian defenders were no match against the powerful 20,000 man Japanese invasion force that overwhelmed the garrison on January 23, 1942. Quickly transformed into a gigantic Japanese army and naval base, Rabaul was manned by 10,000 troops and looked very much like an impregnable fortress. Five airfields serviced 300 airplanes (many of them the dreaded **Zeros**); over 300 anti-aircraft weapons; 43 costal guns for harbor defense; and 20 searchlights to help protect the coastal waters. Beyond question, it was the most heavily defended enemy target in the Southwest Pacific.

Palmer grew up in the small town of Tyler in southwestern Minnesota during the Great Depression. Though times were tough, this fifth child of six children was imbued with a strong sense of self-worth by his Methodist parents. "We were only short of money," he often said, " but never poor in spirit." Instilled with a strong competitive spirit, he was a star high school football and basketball player.

In 1941, the 19-year old Palmer was driving trucks loaded with heavy farm equipment between Minneapolis and Chicago. His hefty salary of $75.00 a week enabled him to set aside substantial sums of money for him to reach his coveted goal of a college education. Life on the whole looked pretty good.

And then the Japanese struck Pearl Harbor and Palmer's world quickly changed. Though he was shocked by the terrible reality of war, he saw an opportunity to do things he had never done before, places to go, things to see, and, perhaps, get some training that would equip him for life. He showed up the next day (December 8) at an Army Recruiting Station, pointedly telling the recruiter that his goal was to serve his country as a fighter pilot in the Army Air Corps. Those hopes were quickly dashed when he was informed he must have two years of college (the rules at that time) and his mother's permission to join up. It took Palmer a couple of months to work through the red tape but finally in March 1942 the requirements were modified and he signed up.

There was more frustration when he was denied the opportunity to pursue his coveted goal as a fighter pilot. Instead, he was sent to the Clovis Army Air Field outside Clovis, New Mexico to train to fly the B-24 *Liberator*. Built by Consolidated Aircraft Corporation, the *Liberator* primarily functioned as a long-range strategic bomber. Compared to Boeing's B-17 *Flying Fortress*, it displayed both advantages and disadvantages. It was faster, carried a heavier bomb load, and flew higher on its missions. But on the flip side, it was more difficult to handle, less stable, and not capable of absorbing the same level of battle damage the *Fortress* was able to sustain. A solid hit on the *Liberator's* wing, for instance, usually proved fatal. Still, good pilots like Palmer loved the plane and overlooked its shortcomings.

In the summer of 1943 Palmer was shipped out to Port Moresby, New Guinea, to serve with the 400th Squadron, 90th Bomb Group, Fifth Air Force. Other squadrons making up the 90th included the 319th; 320th; and 321.st

Coming aboard with the "Jolly Rogers"

The 90th adopted the sobriquet "Jolly Rogers" as a tribute to their popular commanding officer, Colonel Art Rogers. Under his energetic leadership, the 90th would distinguish itself as one of the most lethal bombing groups operating in the Pacific during World War II. Their planes were easily identified by a skull and crossed bombs painted on the twin fins of each B-24.

By the time Palmer, now a captain, arrived in New Guinea, the Fifth Air Force had intensified its strikes against Rabaul, in an effort to neutralize the Japanese from disrupting communications between Australian and American forces operating on the New Guinea-New Britain-Solomons line. Though island hopping had proven successful in America's steady march across the Pacific toward the Japanese mainland, Rabaul's powerful shore defenses negated the launching of an allied amphibious operation; hence the military turned to air strikes to neutralize the place.

Each squadron carried a nickname, nose art, and color designs for good luck: 319th, "Obstreperous" (green); 320th, "Moby Dick"(red); 321st, "Bombs Away"(green); and 400th "Black Pirates" (black). The nose art on Palmer's plane ("Twin Nifty's II") depicted a buxom, half-nude pin-up girl. The crew called her the girl back home.

The fellows needed all those good luck symbols and

Flying high above the target area, TWIN NIFTY'S TWO releases her bomb load and heads for home. U.S. Army Photo.

more when they rolled off the airstrip at Nadzab, New Guinea, that fateful Easter Sunday to make yet another daring strike against Rabaul. Back in Minnesota Palmer's parents were in church that day quietly praying for their pilot son out there somewhere in the Pacific. So, equipped with the "Jolly Rogers" insignia on his twin tails, the "girl back home" on his fuselage, and prayers being quietly said back home, Bob Palmer and his crew lifted off and climbed steadily into the heavens.

Tough skies over Rabaul

This time the Japanese seemed to throw up anything available to them at the incoming bombers, which were flying a "loose" formation that day in order to avoid the speedy **Zeros** as much as possible. Encountering what he described as "a hornet's nest" of deadly firepower, Palmer felt a strong fear of imminent death sweep over him as he approached the target. Things quickly got even worse when he was struck by heavy anti-aircraft fire and attacked by **Zeros** that seemed to swarm all over his plane. Still, he was able to drop his bomb load, turn around, and head home. How he got out of there in one piece remains a mystery—and a miracle—to this day.

But the fight to survive was not quite over. Just as

he thought things had settled down, Palmer was shocked to discover that his right landing gear was damaged and part of the rudder ripped off. Too, the No. 3 engine was virtually destroyed and began burning. The No. 4 engine had also taken a hard hit and was of little use. The lives of the young men on board now depended solely on Palmer and co-pilot Bill Parks, as they faced the almost insurmountable task of safely getting "Twin Nifties" back to base. The bomber shook terribly and wind whistled freely through the over 250 bullet holes put there by the **Zeros**.

Under their steady hands, however, "Twin-Nifty's" proved a tough old girl and refused to give up or go down as she lumbered on for what seemed like an interminable period of time. "It was a test of my sense of survival," Palmer said. He and Parks pledged that if the plane could sputter, they would improvise something that would bring her in a fairly intact condition.

When their home base finally appeared in the distance, Palmer ordered his crew to bail out to lighten the load. Then he stood on the left rudder to keep the plane from veering off to the right while Parks took over the controls. Down they came expecting a crash landing. Instead, they skidded across a long stretch of

Palmer; second from left, and his crew members. Co-pilot Bill Parks is on Palmer's right.
U.S. Army Photo

heavy kunai grass, which gave them the sensation off plopping down on a bale of hay. For this courageous feat, Palmer was awarded the Distinguished Flying Cross.

Palmer soon adjusted to a succession of combat missions, flying 76 in all. Japanese flyers, he concluded, were woefully lacking in pilot smarts as the war wore on because they usually came in at 12 o'clock high, with the intention of ramming if they were not able to knock out the guns of the bombers. Eventually fewer and fewer intercepting **Zeros** showed up and things got much easier over the target. Officially, the Army credited "Twin-Nifty's" with shooting down eight enemy planes, though the count was much higher by Palmer's estimation.

In August 1945 Palmer was stationed at Ie Shime (where the noted war correspondent Ernie Pyle lost his life) to prepare for the anticipated invasion of the Japanese mainland. He knew his former missions would pale into insignificance with what lay ahead. But the dreaded invasion never came. Atomic bombs

were dropped on Hiroshima and Nagasaki and the war was abruptly over to Palmer's relief.

But Bob Palmer's courageous story doesn't end there. Retiring from the service as a major, he served during the postwar period as commanding officer of a squadron in the Combat Replacement Center. Using his GI Bill to good advantage, he graduated with honors from college and medical school. For many years he was a beloved and well known practicing family physician in Indianapolis, Indiana.

Harboring many memories of World War II, this youthful 86 year-old was proud to be part of the "Greatest Generation." "I often think of that period as our finest hour, when our country was united for the common good," he once said. "There will never be another one like it."

As this book was being prepared, Bob Palmer made his final flight beyond the distant horizons after sustaining a massive stroke in December 2009.

Chapter VIII

Alex Vraciu: *Sky Full of "Hellcats"*

Vraciu proudly displays his number of kills (19) as he climbs aboard his HELLCAT fighter.
Courtesy Alex Vraciu.

Naval air ace Alex Vraciu has to be considered one of the luckiest men to have survived World War II. Consider the following: serving on six carriers (two of which were torpedoed), he survived two ditchings, two parachute jumps, and a close call when he was almost captured by the Japanese.

For four months in 1944 Vraciu was the Navy's leading air ace. During the war he shot down 19 enemy planes, destroyed 21 more on the ground, and sank an enemy ship. That's not a bad record for a young fellow who was the son of immigrant Romanian parents and grew up in East Chicago,

Indiana.

A May 1941 graduate of Greencastle, Indiana's DePauw University, Vraciu enlisted in the United States Navy one month later. Sensing that a war was looming just over the horizon, he entered naval flight training just prior to Pearl Harbor. Trained to fly the Grumman F4F *Wildcat*, he received his wings in August 1942. He was temporarily attached to the *USS Wolverine*, a freshwater aircraft carrier that operated on Lake Michigan and was used to train naval pilots in carrier takeoffs and landings.

Arriving in the Pacific combat zone, Vraciu's ready smile and engaging personality belied a tough-minded, no non-sense streak that drove him to the outer limits of air combat, much of it fought in close quarters. One man who instinctively recognized his aerial ability was Lieutenant Commander Edward H. "Butch," O'Hare, was commanding officer of Fighting Squadron 3. Having bagged five Japanese planes in one engagement, O'Hare was already a household name to many Americans.

During a five month stint as O'Hare's wingman, Vraciu shot down his first enemy plane, a Japanese Zero fighter, over Wake Island in October 1943. The taste of combat suited him quite well and a few days later he took out a **Betty** bomber over Tarawa. On January 29, 1944, he made "ace" when he downed three more **Bettys** over Kwajalein.

Flying off the *USS Intrepid,* Vraciu participated in a strike by 72 *Hellcats* in the first Truk Raid on February 16, 1944. Sweeping over the Japanese bases, the *Hellcats* unleashed an unremitting fire in the air and on the airstrips. Vraciu's kills that day included three **Zeros** and one Rufe (Japanese seaplane). Unfortunately, *Intrepid* was torpedoed by a Japanese Kate bomber during the night and was forced to withdraw from the combat zone.

With *Intrepid* undergoing repairs at Hunter's Point, California, Vraciu's VF-6 squadron also returned to the states. After requesting the Navy to let him remain in combat, he was assigned to Fighter Squadron 16 aboard the carrier *USS Lexington*. Nicknamed the "Blue Ghost," the newly commissioned ship weighed 33,000 tons and boasted a 910 foot flight deck. Vraciu downed two more **Zeros** during the second Truk raid on April 29, then got his twelfth kill north of Saipan on June 12. Two days later he sank a large merchant ship with a direct hit on its stern.

Great Marianas Turkey Shoot

Though these feats were highly impressive, what Vraciu did on June 19 still boggles one's mind. He literally took control of the skies during the epic Battle of the Philippine Sea, June 19-20, 1944. Dubbed the "Great Marianas Turkey Shoot," the battle ended up as a lop-sided victory for the Americans.

Island hopping by that time had brought America's military forces all the way across the vast Pacific Ocean to the Marianas Islands. Should Japan lose control of that crucial piece of real estate, only Iwo Jima and Okinawa lay between the irresistible Americans and the Japanese mainland. Consequently, the Japanese high command decided to go on the offensive and attack the United States Pacific Fleet before the expected assault began. Vice Admiral Jisaboro Ozawa would head the operation.

On the surface the armada that the Japanese pieced together looked quite formidable. There were five large carriers, four light carriers, five battleships, and a generous mix of cruisers, destroyers, and oilers. This impressive display of firepower, however, was greatly offset by the fact that mostly green pilots would fly the planes.

By now, however, America had in her possession the Grumman F6F-3 *Hellcat*, regarded as the world's greatest carrier fighter plane. The presence of the *Hellcat* in the Pacific meant that America could send hundreds of aircraft into the skies that far exceeded anything the Japanese could put up. Flown by Navy and Marine Corps pilots, the *Hellcat*, which did not go into service until August 1943, destroyed 5,171 enemy aircraft in the air and on the ground during the final two years of the war.

Itching for a good fight, Lieutenant J.G. Alex Vraciu would be at the controls of one of those **Cats** on June 19, 1944.

On June 15 American submarines spotted the Japanese Fleet heading toward the Marianas chain of islands. It didn't take a crash course in rocket science to convince Admiral Raymond Spruance (Midway), commander of the U.S. 5th Fleet, that a major battle was at hand. Incidentally, Spruance's flagship at that time was the ill-fated heavy cruiser *Indianapolis* that

On board USS LEXINGTON an exuberant Vraciu holds up six fingers to indicate number of Japanese planes he splashed in one engagement at the "Great Marianas Turkey Shoot." Courtesy Alex Vraciu

would be lost at sea during the closing hours of the war.

On the afternoon of June 18, Vice Admiral Marc Mitscher (Doolittle's Raid) aboard his flagship *Lexington* prepared Task Force 58, which was part of the 5th Fleet, to meet the expected Japanese attack near Saipan. This powerful force included seven heavy carriers and eight light carriers imbedded within five Task Groups that were surrounded by a heavy screen of cruisers and destroyers. TG 58.7 alone showcased seven battleships, among them the celebrated 58,000-tonners *New Jersey* and *Iowa*. Indeed, things had changed for the better for America's Navy in the Pacific since Midway.

With its massive amounts of armor, firepower, and horsepower, this powerful naval force moved quickly to force a showdown with the approaching enemy force. The Americans had come too far and too long to back off. If the Japanese wanted a fight, they were about to have one.

At 8:30 a.m. Ozawa opened the battle by launching eight torpedo equipped **Jills**, Japan's standard torpedo bomber, 43 **Zero** fighter-bombers, and 14 **Zero** fighters, all flown by pilots with six or less months experience. The second launch came 16 minutes later, this time with 27 **Jills**, 48 **Zeros**, and 53 **Judy** bombers. Two more launches would come later in the day.

Vraciu splashes six Japanese planes

To counter the initial move by the Japanese, there arose that morning from the various American carrier decks over 200 *Hellcats*, all of them flown by

A rare never before published photo shows Admiral Marc Mitscher congratulating Naval Ace Vraciu aboard Flagship LEXINGTON shortly after the "Turkey Shoot." Courtesy Alex Vraciu.

seasoned pilots each of whom could boast of at least two years flying experience. Vraciu led the second division in the group of 12 **Hellcats** that launched from **Lexington**. True to their nickname, the Cats pounced on the incoming force with a vengeance. In little time, enemy planes began to fall from the heavens as though swatted by a giant fly flap. The Americans flew, soared, and fought with an almost reckless abandon against what was obviously an inferior attacking force.

At about 20,000 feet Vraciu spotted a large, rambling mass of at least 50 planes approximately 2,000 feet below him on the port side heading for the American Fleet. This was a fighter pilot's dream and Vraciu reacted with alacrity. Streaking beneath the formation, he quickly dropped one **Judy** into the sea.

Pulling up, he spotted two more **Judys** that were slightly detached from the main body. This time coming in from the rear he sent one down in flames. Dipping the **Hellcat's** wing, he slid over on the one that was slightly in front of him and quickly disposed of it. The rear gunner of the enemy plane was still firing away as his plane made a sharp arc downward and disappeared..

Vraciu later recalled that the sky at that moment revealed "an incredible sight, full of smoke, tracers, debris, and bits of planes." Just then he saw another enemy plane breaking out of the formation. One short burst from his gun sent number four spiraling downward.

Meanwhile several **Jills** and **Judys** had penetrated through the outer screen and were about to peel off and release their bombs. His adrenalin now flowing at the max, Vraciu locked onto the one closest to him, touched his gun trigger, and saw the plane explode in pieces. He caught the next—and final one—just as it began its dive. Another burst of fire from Vraciu's gun and the plane split to pieces with a "sky-shaking explosion." Splash number six for the intrepid Hoosier.

Only one **Judy** remained but not for long. A direct hit from anti-aircraft firing from down below quickly erased it from the battle scene. As things quieted down, Vraciu had a few moments to look around. As far as his eyes could see there was only a "sky full of **Hellcats**."

Vraciu was invited to Corpus Christi, Texas in 1992 to Participate in the formal opening of his old carrier LEXINGTON as a floating Museum of Naval History. Assisting in the ceremonies was Angie Sisk, Miss Texas. U.S.A. Author's Collection

Alex Vraciu had taken out six enemy planes in only eight minutes, —all in a day's work, he would say. He got another **Zero** the next day, his last enemy kill during the war.

By any stretch of the imagination, America had achieved an overwhelming victory during the "Turkey Shoot." The enemy lost three irreplaceable carriers, 600 planes, and six ships heavily damaged—losses it could not replace at this stage of the war. By contrast, our losses totaled 123 planes, though the crews of 80 were later rescued.

Now an American icon in his own right, Vraciu was returned to the States with his air group. However, when a War Bond Tour looked imminent he talked his way out of the tour and returned, instead, to the **Lexington** in the combat area. It was during this assignment that his incredible luck finally ran out. On December 14, 1944, he was shot down by enemy anti-aircraft fire while strafing an airfield adjacent to Clark Field in the Philippines during his second mission.

Parachuting to safety, he spent the next five weeks hiding out with Filipino guerrillas, who gave him the honorary rank of Brevet Major and placed him in charge of 180 men. When he finally got the group to an American camp, Vraciu was sporting a Luger and carrying a Japanese sword.

No longer permitted to remain in the combat zone, Vraciu was assigned to the Naval Air Test Center Patuxent River, Maryland, for the last four months of the war, helping evaluate tactical performances of both United States and enemy aircraft.

In the post-war period he was given command of Fighter Squadron 51. A retired banker, he presently resides in Danville, California. As one of the few surviving American fighter pilots of World War II, he carries many memories of those thrilling moments when split second timing determined whether one would live or die. Though that heady June day over the Pacific has long since faded into the past and is little more than a blip in our national consciousness, Vraciu will never forget his exhilaration of seeing a sky filled with **Hellcats**.

Commander Alexander Vraciu in front of a FJ-3 "Fury" like the one in which he won top honors at the 1957 Naval Air Weapons Meet in El Centra, California. - U.S. Navy Photo

Chapter IX

George H.W. Bush: *Chichi Jima*

Japan's surprise attack on Pearl Harbor, found 17 year old George Herbert Walker Bush a student leader in his senior year at the prestigious Phillips Academy in Andover, Massachusetts. Quite popular with both students and faculty, Bush was captain of both the baseball and soccer teams, playing manager of the basketball team, and a member of the student government. He had already been accepted for fall admittance at Yale, his wealthy father's (Prescott Bush) alma mater.

Despite his many material advantages in life, Bush typified many of that era's young men who felt a sense of urgency to defend their country during war. Consequently, attending Yale and later pursuing a lucrative career would have to wait. Upon graduating from Phillips six months later on his 18th birthday, he enlisted in the United States Navy and headed down to the University of North Carolina in Chapel Hill for pre-flight training. On June 9, 1943, three days short of turning 19, he became the Navy's youngest pilot after completing his flight training at Corpus Christi Naval Air Station. He was commissioned "Ensign" in the United States Naval Reserve.

Bush's primary aircraft, the Grumman *Avenger* Torpedo Bomber (TBM), carried three crew members: the pilot in the forward seat, the turret gunner behind him, and below, facing aft, the radio/tail gunner. Nicknamed the "Pregnant Turkey," the huge plane was cumbersome and slow. Despite all that, Bush liked it because it performed extremely well when releasing bombs, depth charges, and torpedoes against stationary installations, surface ships, and submarines.

Assigned to Torpedo Squadron VT-51, Bush boarded the light carrier *USS San Jacinto* that September and headed for combat duty in the Pacific. In the spring of 1944 the *San Jacinto* joined Task Force 58, Vice Admiral Marc A. Mitscher's fast carrier outfit that was operating near the Japanese held Marianas Islands in the western Pacific. Created by Mitscher,

Seated in the cockpit of his AVENGER, Bush maps out his target for the day. U.S. Navy Photo

TF 58 was attached to the U.S. 5th Fleet under Admiral Raymond Spruance, thus making it the Navy's major Pacific striking force during the latter part of the war.

On June 15, 1944, American submarines spotted Vice-Admiral Jisaburo Ozawa's large flotilla of carriers, battleships, cruisers, destroyers, and oil tankers headed toward the Marianas. A few days earlier U.S. carrier planes had initiated a series of small strikes on the islands, to the surprise of the Japanese who were expecting the Americans to foray farther south, either in the Caroline or Palaus islands. Consequently, the Marianas were only lightly defended.

Great Marianas Turkey Shoot

Convinced that a major sea battle was at hand, Spruance sent Mitscher's TF 58 over to Saipan to block any possible enemy threat that might come from that direction. Mitscher's formidable armada consisted of seven heavy carriers, eight light carriers, seven battleships, 79 other ships, and 28 submarines. Carrying over 900 planes, piloted by some of the Navy's best pilots, TF 58 gave the Americans a decided edge over the weaker, less experienced Japanese airmen, who would pilot approximately 750 mostly obsolete carrier-based and land-based planes. Thus, the stage was set for perhaps the greatest and certainly the most decisive naval battle of World War II.

The two forces clashed on June 19-20 in the Battle of the Philippine Sea in a no holds bared contest that resulted in a lop-sided American victory. Mitscher launched air patrol planes at 5:30 a.m. on June 19, followed moments later by *Hellcats* taking off from *Belleau Wood* to intercept Japanese fighters approaching from airfields in Guam. In short order the *Hellcats* shot down 35 enemy aircraft, leaving little doubt that the Americans had clearly taken control of the skies.

There was no let up in the aerial action throughout the day. Wave after wave of incoming enemy fighters were easily plucked off by charged-up pilots flying *Hellcats* and *Avengers.* Their adrenalin flowing to the max, the pilots returned to their ships only long

The US SAN JACINTO was originally a 10,000 ton light cruiser which was converted into a light carrier. The ship's narrow flight deck made it difficult to land planes. U.S. Navy Photo.

enough to refuel, grab a sandwich, sip some juice, check the blackboard, and inform intelligence officers of their success. Then they dashed back to their planes to try to improve their score. One observer noted that the pilots attitude indicated that "they were engaged not in a battle at all but in some especially fast and exciting game, like polo or hockey." One ecstatic *Lexington* pilot yelled out: "Hell, this is like an old-time turkey shoot." The term stuck and the epic battle is forever remembered as the "Great Mariana's Turkey Shoot."

Meanwhile, enemy dive bombers had effectively pinned down *San Jacinto*, making the *Avengers* on board especially vulnerable because of the high explosives they carried. It was critical that they get off the ship as soon as possible. Seated atop virtual powder kegs that could explode at any moment, Bush and his fellow pilots waited impatiently until the besieged ship finally was able to maneuver itself into a position to launch the planes.

Shortly after getting airborne Bush's oil system was struck, causing the pressure to plummet and requiring him to ditch in the ocean. He coolly slid the stricken plane onto the rough water and released the life raft, thus enabling him and his two crew members to scramble to safety. Thirty minutes later the men were rescued by the destroyer *Clarence K. Bronson*. Bush and another pilot shared credit in sinking a small cargo ship during the melee, resulting in Bush's promotion to lieutenant junior grade.

The Japanese continued to take heavy losses the next day—losses that were impossible for them to replace at that stage of the war. To illustrate how one-sided the battle was, *Yorktown's* four air groups, dubbed the "Flying Circus," shot down 50 enemy planes without sustaining even one bullet hole in their own planes. By comparison Japanese losses were astronomical: three carriers and two oilers sunk, six ships heavily damaged, and 600 planes destroyed. Mitscher's losses totaled 123 planes and no ships destroyed or severely damaged. Eighty flight crews that ditched in the sea, including Bush's, were later picked up.

Though plenty of tough fighting lay ahead at places like Iwo Jima and Okinawa, America was marching steadily across the western Pacific toward the Japanese mainland. However, with the Marianas now firmly under its control, the United States was in a position to build airfields large enough to accommodate the giant B-29s that would soon strike deeply into the heart of the Empire.

Bush's close call with death

Though Bush, now 20, had performed well during five months of service in the Pacific, he soon faced a challenge so great that it would become a defining moment in his life. With over 40 missions under his belt, he had proven his mettle by flying against heavy antiaircraft fire over places like Guam, Wake Island, Saipan, and Marcus Island. At Chichi Jima he would face much heavier odds.

Chichi Jima in the Bonian Islands today is only a small blip in the study of the Pacific War. In those days it posed a dangerous threat to the American advance toward Japan. Claimed by Japan since 1875, its small garrison had been substantially increased since December 1941. Since it was located only 700 miles from the mainland, it posed a stumbling block to the American advance across the Pacific. Conversely, as the Americans drew ever nearer, Chichi Jima, including Haha Jima and Iwo Jima, became more vulnerable to being overrun. Consequently, by 1944 a naval base and antiaircraft batteries had been installed. A heavily protected radio installation erected on Chichi Jima could quickly alert the Japanese mainland of incoming bomber flights. Obviously, this facility must be taken out to lessen the risk to the new wave of bombing by the B-29s.

And there was something else about Chichi Jima that both concerned and frightened the Americans should any of our men be captured. Since June 15, 1944, when American planes first struck Chichi Jima, many of our planes had been brought down and the pilots captured. Word had gotten out that prisoners were beheaded and their bodies used for bayonet practice. Koreans who were forced into slave labor on the island reported after the war that they saw captured pilots cut into pieces and eaten by their sadistic captors. All things considered, Chichi Jima posed a formidable problem to any pilot who attacked it. No record exists that any pilot captured on Chichi Jima ever returned.

On September 1, 1944, heavy ground antiaircraft fire repelled Bush's squadron from dismantling the radio complex. This was no time to let up on the pressure, so the next day the Americans were at it again. The target for the day was to knock out Asahi Station No. 6, a 6,400 square foot power plant, which operated a 3,600 square foot transmitter and 200 foot high radio antenna. Bush was included in a four plane squadron assigned to carry out the dangerous mission. His crew included Radioman Second Class John Delaney and Gunner Lieutenant J.G. William Gardner "Ted" White, the squadron ordnance officer. White wanted to go along to check out the *Avenger's* weapons system. Bush warned him that the flight could be pretty rough but White persisted. Finally, permission was given by Commander Don Melvin for White to substitute for the regular gunner, Lee Nadeau.

At 7:15 a.m. the squadron lifted off from the deck of *San Jacinto*, each plane weighted down with four 500 pound bombs. At 8:15 the lead and second planes began their glide-bombing runs. Bush's turn came up on the third drop. By then a punishing antiaircraft bombardment caught Bush in the crosshairs. Still, he held steady and began a 60 degree angle bomb run from 8,000 feet. Halfway down the *Avenger* took a fatal hit in its engine. "Suddenly there was a jolt," Bush later recalled, "as if a massive fist had crunched into the belly of the plane. Smoke poured into the cockpit and I could see flames rippling across the crease of the wing, edging toward the fuel tanks. I stayed with the dive, homed in on the target, unloaded our four 500 pound bombs and pulled away, heading for the sea."

With his plane covered with heavy smoke and rapidly losing altitude, Bush could not see his controls and flames were spreading along the wings toward the fuel tanks. He told Delaney and White to bail out. One man, who was already either injured or dead, never made it. The other one, who was not identified, managed to get out but fell to his death when his chute failed to open.

In addition to Bush, four other aviators were rescued by the FINBACK. Kneeling from left to right, Thomas Keene, Bush, James W. Beckham, James T. Stovall, and John H. Doherty. Standing are FINBACK crewmembers who assisted in the rescue.

At about 2,000 feet, Bush prematurely unfastened his seat belt and jumped out of the doomed plane. He yanked the ripcord too quickly and banged his head against the plane's tail, causing a bloody gash above his head. Though momentarily stunned, he instinctively began to unbuckle himself on the way down. Striking the water, he slipped out of the harness about four miles northeast of Chichi Jima.

More problems arose when a powerful ocean swell swept away his parachute's life raft. Fortunately, Commander Melvin, flying 500 feet above him, saw Bush's plight, dropped him a yellow one-man raft, and contacted the **USS Finback**, a rescue submarine in the area. Melvin then dipped his wings to indicate the raft's location. Bush swam over to it, inflated it, and climbed on board. To his horror, the strong ocean

After being shot down and almost captured by the Japanese, Bush was rescued
On the starboard bow of the submarine FINBACK. U.S. Navy Photo.

current was steadily carrying him toward Chichi Jima's eastern shore and certain capture. Melvin and a second pilot, Milt Moore, began strafing enemy vessels coming out to pick up Bush. They sank several boats and drove the others back to the shore before returning to base to refuel. The future president's guardian angels were certainly with him that fateful day.

His head pounding from its strong lick, Bush waited three hours before the *Finback* finally surfaced and he was rescued. The timing could not have come at a better moment, for by now other boats, aware that the cover planes were gone, were coming out to pick him up. Once safely aboard he was joined by downed crews from other flights. Sadly, Delaney and White were never found.

Bush spent 30 days aboard the *Finback*, one of the Navy's largest submarines, while it continued stalking and sinking enemy vessels, as well as rescuing other downed pilots. During that time the young airman had time to reflect on why God had spared him in the face of imminent death. At Pearl Harbor he declined

an offer to take a month's leave, preferring, instead, to complete his tour of duty on the *San Jacinto* and fly 12 more missions. In all, he flew 58 combat missions during the war, spent 1,228 flight hours in the air, and made 126 carrier landings. He was reassigned to the Norfolk Navy Yard to instruct young pilots in the intricacies of aerial combat. Following his honorable discharge at the end of the war, he enrolled at Yale University.

Bush was awarded the "Distinguished Flying Cross" and three air medals. In part, the DFC Citation read: "Although his plane was hit and set afire at the beginning of his dive, he continued his plunge toward the target and succeeded in scoring damaging bomb hits before bailing out of the craft. His courage and devotion to duty were in keeping with the highest traditions of the United States Naval Reserve."

In later life Bush recalled his war years as a "sobering" experience that "broadened my horizons." In that regard, our 41st President is just like any other World War II veteran.

President George Bush with Elbert Watson at the White House, 1992.
Courtesy Susan Biddle, White House Photo. Author's Collection.

66

Chapter X

Sergeant Soochow: *P.O.W. Survivor*

Perhaps every reader of this book is familiar with the names of Jimmie Doolittle, Paul Tibbets, "Pappy" Boyington, "Butch" O'Hare, and Alex Vraciu, to name a few of the authentic American heroes of World War II. But how about Soochow, Chips, Lassie II, Butter, and Jeep? Nicknames? No, these were pets adopted by men who served in the forward areas of combat. Loyal and true to their masters and military units, these animals, and many others like them, experienced the war up close. Like their human buddies, they took danger in stride, accepted risks, and gave their best despite difficult circumstances.

Pets have served with our country's armed forces dating back to the American Revolution. In times of war, particularly, they often bring a touch of humanity to war's inhumane conditions; befriend lonely men far away from home and under constant threat of death; and give unconditional love to frightened soldiers. Only a lengthy book could properly detail the lives of the great pet heroes of World War II. The few ones noted here merely illustrate the magnitude of the sacrifice many of them made to help win the war and thus protect our nation's freedom.

Lieutenant-Colonel John W. "Wild Bill" Crump developed one of the most unusual relationships that ever existed between a man and his pet. While undergoing his flight training near Bruning, Nebraska, he adopted a two weeks old wolf pup from a Nebraska farmer. Named Jeep, the pup accompanied Crump to Baton Rouge, Louisiana, for P-47 *Thunderbolt* training, then overseas when Crump's unit was sent to Martlesham Heath Aerodrome. There the men of the 360th Fighter Squadron adopted Jeep as their official mascot, giving him field grade treatment and

Bill "Wild" Bill Crump and his flying partner "Jeep" return from yet another combat mission.
U.S. Army Photo.

complete run of the base.

Jeep flew five combat missions as Crump's "co-pilot," one of which was the highly dangerous "Market Garden" strike in the Netherlands on September 18, 1944. The 8th Air Force sent up several fighter groups that day to take out flak positions prior to and during the jumps. Of the approximately 350 fighters that bombed and straffed targets in the Nijmegen and Arnhem areas, only Crump's plane had a "co-pilot"—Jeep.

Crump had just neutralized an artillery emplacement when he unexpectedly drew heavy fire. As he pushed over with his **Thunderbolt**, the pressure was so intense that Jeep was lifted up from the cockpit floor and began floating in air between Crump and the gunsight, clawing to gain a paw hold. Undistracted, Crump headed over to some nearby treetops for cover, while at the same time retrieving the animal and slipping its collar ring over the "Jug's" hydraulic pump handle.

Unfortunately, Jeep fell victim to ground traffic, killed, ironically, by an Army jeep. His final mission came on September 23, 1944, when portions of the 82nd and 101st Airborne Divisions and the Polish 1st Brigade were air-dropped and landed at two zones in the Nijmegan area. Fourteen 8th Air Force groups flew bombing and strafing missions that day. Jeep was buried with full military honors at Playford Hall, a former Eagle Squadron billet. A "missing man" formation roared high above his courtyard grave, and Crump himself gave his pal a final salute with a spine-tingling low-altitude victory roll.

Crump logged 311 combat hours in 77 missions, which consisted primarily of strafing, flak busting, and escorting. Retiring from the service as a lieutenant-colonel, he returned to his hometown of Edmonds, Washington, where he became a successful businessman and civic leader prior to his death in 2007. Over the years, however, he never forgot the faithful animal who loved and served him during the war. To assure that Jeep would always be remembered, Crump placed the little coyote's medical records, coyote tags, and pictures in the Edmonds History Museum where they are on public display today.

"Butter" was trained to parachute with troops

Then there was Butter, a stray dog who took a liking to the men of the 434th Troop Carrier Group, 72nd Troop Carrier Squadron that was activated on February 9, 1943, and trained to operate C-47s with the Ninth Air Force. Unable to bear leaving the little dog behind, Gerald Higginbottom gathered her up tightly in his arms as the group was departing for England the following October and took her along.

Overseas, Butter never lacked for companionship, slept in the barracks, and flew with the men on many of their evacuation and combat missions. She was even outfitted with a special chute that had a static line attached to it so she could jump if it became necessary to bail out. Her campaigns included Normandy, Northern France, Rhineland, the Ardennes, and Alsace. In appreciation of her meritorious service she was given a "dress uniform" and made an honorary sergeant.

Sadly, Butter also came to an untimely end. On June 24, 1945, the 72nd left France to return home. Arriving in French West Africa, the unit was met by Military Police who confiscated Butter despite loud protests by the men.

Fourth Marine "Soochow" survived Japanese imprisonment

Perhaps the most amazing and gripping story to come out of World War II about pet loyalty and tenacity is that of Marine "Sergeant Soochow," a sad eyed multi-breed dog, who took up with the 4th Marines, or China Marines, in Shanghai, China, prior to the outbeak of the war. The Marines, who had been in China since 1927, were responsible for guarding bridges over Soochow Creek to prevent hostilities between China and invading Japanese forces from spilling over into the international section of the city.

One dark, rainy night, the small white and brown mongrel dog straggled into one of the Marine outposts and made it his home. Other dogs that tried to follow suit caught the brunt of his wrath. Barking, growling, and snapping at the intruders, the little orphan left no doubt that this was his post and other mongrels were not welcome.

The tough-minded, though soft-hearted, Marines fed, housed, and quickly spoiled the little mutt. Members

PFC Soochow leads his fellow China Marines to their assignments in pre-war Shanghai, China.

of B Company formally adopted him as their mascot and named him Soochow after the creek they were guarding. Never weighing more than 35 pounds, Soochow easily became a familiar figure on the base as he pranced about freely in his specially designed uniform. He even chomped down sirloin steaks and regularly hung out with his Marine buddies when they had nights out on the town.

Then everything abruptly changed! In late November 1941, with war rapidly approaching, the 4th Marines were transferred from Shanghai down to the Philippines. Refusing to leave their pal Soochow behind, his fellow Marines smuggled him aboard their ship, the **S.S. *President Harrison***. One week after they reached Olongapo, the U.S. Navy base at the northwestern tip of Bataan Peninsula, the Japanese struck Pearl Harbor and the war was on.

One month later on January 7, 1942, the Japanese began their anticipated siege of the peninsula. The 4th Marines were charged with the defense of Corregidor, thought to be an impregnable island fortress at the entrance to Manila Bay. B Company was assigned to the eastern, or tail section, of the tadpole shaped island. Soochow quickly learned the

value of using a foxhole when bombs and artillery shells began raining down on Corregidor over the next four months. Too, his keen sense of hearing enabled him to alert his fellow Marines to incoming enemy planes long before their detection was picked up by the primitive radar systems in use at that time.

When Corregidor fell on May 12, 1942, Soochow was also taken prisoner. For some inexplicable reason the Japanese guards permitted the Marines to keep and take care of him. PFC Bob Snyder, his principal caretaker, took him off the island to Bilibid Prison in Manila and later to the infamous prisoner of war camp at Cabanatuan. Amazingly, during the next 32 months Snyder kept Soochow alive by grubbing for grains of rice or spoonfuls of soup provided by other prisoners. It boggles the mind to think of the extraordinary love and devotion given to the mongrel by ill and dying Marines, considering the fact that they were barely subsisting themselves on nothing more than starvation rations.

In November 1944, Snyder was transferred from Cabanatuan to Japan, leaving Soochow under the care of remaining prisoners. Unfortunately, his unmarked ship was sunk by a U.S. Navy plane near

Safe at home, PFC Soochow poses with fellow Marine "Pappy" Wells shortly after their release from a Japanese POW camp. U.S. Marine Photo

Formosa and most of the men on board perished, including Snyder.

When the last group of able-bodied prisoners were returned from Cabanatuan to Bilibid, Soochow was among them. A couple of weeks later, on February 4, 1945, American Rangers liberated the little pooch and his 17 surviving Marines. An Army Transport ship was to return the sick and emaciated men back to the States, but a hitch developed when the captain refused to allow Soochow on board. Though bone-tired from their years of captivity, the incensed men raised such a howl that the Navy itself flew him home, accompanied by Technical Sergeant Paul J. "Pappy" Wells.

Well aware of what the little dog had endured during his long imprisonment, the Marines made sure that he lived out his remaining years with dignity and respect. Assigned to the Marine Recruit Depot in San Diego, California, Soochow was an instant celebrity and a greatly beloved and pampered base mascot. He was regularly seen out on the Parade Field trotting alongside his fellow "Boots," or snuggling close to another Marine in the barracks.

Soochow's military honors included the following ribbons and medals: Asiatic-Pacific Campaign, Good Conduct, World War Victory and American Defense. A base parade was held in his honor on October 29, 1946, his ninth birthday. All agreed that he had fulfilled the Marine motto: "Always Faithful."

On April 21, 1948, Sergeant Soochow, former China Marine, defender of Corregidor, and prisoner of war, slipped through the thin line of worlds that separates this one from the next one to join his old buddies whom he had lost for a while but never forgot. Today, visitors to the Recruit Depot will find his well kept grave marker prominently displayed on Guadalcanal Street.

Quite often we take for granted the daily presence of those little pets in and around our home who give us such unselfish love and devotion. Perhaps we should take an occasional second look. There just might be a Jeep, a Butter, a Chips, or just perhaps, a Soochow nipping at our heartstrings.

Soochow's gravesite on Guadalcanal Street, Marine Corps Recruit Depot, San Diego, California.

SOOCHOW

Once a Marine, always a Marine, Semper Fi.

Chapter XI

Bert Shepard: *Hero In The Air—And On The Bases*

Two fellows who never quit despite their handicaps. Bert Shepard and Pete Gray both made it to the majors in 1945.

Robert E. "Bert" Shepard was a high-spirited, gifted young athlete. Like many small town youngsters who grew up between the two world wars, he dreamed of one day playing baseball in the major leagues. Born on June 28, 1920, in Dana, Indiana (also the hometown of the noted World War II correspondent Ernie Pyle), Bert's athletic prowess was well known throughout the area. He starred in several high school sports; later played semi-pro baseball; and spent two years in the minor leagues during an era when baseball ruled America's sports world. To become another Babe Ruth, Lou Gehrig, Bob Feller, or Mickey Cochran was the goal of many small town youngsters. Shepard one day would rank right up there with them, of that his many neighborhood

friends were sure.

Then along came World War II and Bert's life changed forever. A true patriot, he enlisted in the Army Air Corps in May, 1942, and reported to Fort Benjamin Harrison near Indianapolis for basic training. Named after President Benjamin Harrison, who lived in Indianapolis and is buried there, the camp was opened in 1908 as a major Induction and Logistical Center for inductees hailing from the Midwest. From there, Bert headed down to Daniel Field, Georgia, a small civilian airport that recently had been converted into a bustling military air base. Upon completing intensive flight training in 1943, he received his wings and was commissioned second lieutenant. Standing 5'11" and weighing 185 pounds, the handsome young athlete exuded the finest physical and moral qualities expected of a United States Army Air Corps officer.

Bert's craving for action was rewarded when he was attached to the 55th Fighter Squadron at Wormingford, Air Field, in Essex County on the eastern side of the United Kingdom. Tracing its history back to August 9, 1917, the 55th was re-designated as a fighter squadron in May 1942, and transitioned to fly the flashy Bell P-39 *Airacobra* and Lockheed P-38 *Lightning*, Bert's primary aircraft.

Not surprisingly, Bert's high energy and love of excitement found their logical outlet as pilot of a plane that boasted *Lightning's* power and maneuverability. Designed in 1937 as a high altitude interceptor aircraft, the *Lightning's* two powerful engines gave it a decided edge over any other fighter in the air during the war. Coincidentally, those two engines gave Bert another plus as a *Lightning* pilot, since they were manufactured at the Allison Engineering Company on the far west side of Indianapolis, Indiana. Established in 1915 by Jim A. Allison, one of the founders of the Indianapolis Motor Speedway, the company originally concentrated on building racing cars for the annual "Indy 500," as well as smaller events around the country.

World War I, however, changed the direction of the thriving, but largely unheralded Hoosier plant. Sensing an opportunity to actively involve itself in the war effort, Allison began producing essential parts for the Hall-Scott and Liberty Aircraft companies, which had been retained by the United States government to manufacture engines for the country's fledgling air force. This successful venture convinced Allison's owners that the time had come for the company to move into a larger market that had worldwide implications. Recognized both for its high standard of workmanship and fine precision work, Allison by 1920 had shelved its auto manufacturing for good.

In the years leading up to World War II, Allison was producing a special bearing used at that time in most of America's aircraft engines, turning out superchargers for the General Electric Company, and providing reduction gears for Navy dirigibles. As a division of General Motors by 1938, Allison, with its 200 person work force, had successfully tested the famous liquid-cooled thoroughbred V1710 12

cylinder aircraft engine at 1,000 hp. The *Lightning* proved a natural fit for the new state of the art engines.

The sleek *Lightning* was so aerodynamically perfect that its landing gear when lowered accounted for 60 per cent of the total drag. If the landing gear were retracted, the entire plane's drag was less than, say, a 27-inch card table flown in the air. Operating under the steady hand of a skilled pilot, the plane's 20mm cannon and four .50 caliber machine guns could emit enough firepower to completely destroy an enemy aircraft in little more than a second. Often finding themselves on the receiving end of such devastating firepower, it is no wonder the Germans dubbed the plane the "fork-tail devil." Allison produced a grand total of 29,862 V1710 engines for the *Lightning* during the war.

The 55th was made up of a feisty bunch of devil-may-care, hotshot airmen, who already had left a significant mark on World War II. Shortly after Pearl Harbor, the unit was rushed to the Aleutians to protect the island group from almost certain attack and capture by rapidly advancing Japanese forces, who were sent forward to strike a knockout blow against the United States. Once that situation was eased, the 55th was deployed to Europe to help lay the foundation for the massive Allied air armada then building up against Germany.

In England the 55th was attached to the Eighth Air Force's ("Mighty Eighth") 66th Fighter Wing. Its primary mission was to escort B-17 *Flying Fortress* bombers in their devastating daylight air assaults on Germany's industrial sites and railroads. These surgical strikes carefully and effectively began carving up the Third Reich. Offering critical assistance in the raids was the *Lightning*, which quickly became a terror in the skies because of its heavy firepower and long range.

For his part, Shepard flew 33 missions in all, one of which was the first daylight raid on Berlin on March 2, 1944. Still, he found time to participate in the 55th's various athletic activities. He helped organize a baseball team and served as its player-manager. With spring just around the corner, some of the fellows cleared off a playing field, laid out a diamond, and began warming up for the opening game scheduled for Sunday afternoon, May 21.

On that day, however, Shepard's "Play Ball" call

turned out to be a double-header of sorts. He volunteered to help bomb an enemy airfield near Ludwiglust, Germany, east of Hamburg, thinking the mission would only be a quick shot (sortie) on the target, giving him ample time to return to base and warm up for his pitching assignment that afternoon. Fickle fate, however, intervened and he never made it back to the field he helped lay out, and which would later bear his name, "Shepard Field."

Austrian doctor saves Shepard's life

As the mission got underway, Bert's adrenalin was pumping a mile a minute as his trusty *Lightning* shot skyward. Approaching the target area, he deftly slid the plane beneath the clouds in order to zero in on his prey. A short blast of his 20 mm cannon and it would all be over, he thought. Then he could head home, sprint from the aircraft to the playing field, and suit up for the big game.

Sadly, the strike at the target didn't quite work out that way. The mission turned out to be no "milk run" assignment. To Bert's surprise, the cocked and ready Germans began pouring heavy anti-aircraft fire into the incoming flights. Well placed missiles effectively honed in on the attacking force. So intense was the reaction down below that the skies were quickly filled with heavy flak (bursting shells), the terror of any airman who was caught over enemy territory.

Despite the wild greeting, Bert completed his mission, veered his plane around and began racing home at a low altitude through increasingly heavy flak filled skies. Suddenly a shell crashed into the cockpit striking his right leg with sledge-hammer impact, shattering his leg and separating it from his foot. As though that were not enough, a moment later another shell struck his head and knocked him senseless.

In what was the first of many miracles to happen to him over the next year, a dazed Bert amazingly collected his wits just long enough to crash land his plane at 380 mph onto some lush, level farm land not far from the outskirts of Ludwiglust. German farmers, incensed over seeing their property ripped apart by the intruder, converged on the scene and would have beaten the battered airman to death had not 26 year old Lieutenant Ladislaus Loidl, an Austrian physician serving in the German Luftwaffe, showed up with two armed soldiers in time to disperse the outraged mob.

Loidl's cursory examination of the completely unconscious Bert revealed that Shepard's mangled right leg was almost severed from his body. His chances for survival appeared quite slim to Loidl, unless he was quickly treated in a medical facility. Since Loidl's nearby emergency hospital did not perform amputations, he rushed Shepard to a local hospital. The colonel in charge there adamantly refused to admit an enemy combatant, regardless of his condition. Refusing to give up the fight to save Bert's life, Loidl telephoned the German Air Ministry in Berlin and spoke directly to the general in command. The colonel was overruled and the operation went ahead without further delay.

Over the next several weeks, a groggy Bert wandered in and out of consciousness under the watchful care of Dr. Loidl. Finally, he woke up for good in the local hospital minus his right leg, which had been amputated eleven inches below the knee. His banged up head still ached but, thankfully, he was alive.

Several months passed before Shepard was discharged from the hospital, and incarcerated in Staglag IX-C, a prison camp near Meiningen in central Germany. Again, the miracles that accompanied Bert on his long sojourn through the dark night of adversity held out. Servicing a number of sub-camps in the general area, Staglag IX-C offered its POWs a large, well-equipped, highly serviceable hospital. It was operated by competent prison inmates hailing from Britain, Canada, and New Zealand. Had the decision been left to him, Bert, under the circumstances, could not have selected a better prison facility than that of Staglag IX-C.

Left with plenty of time to pondered his future, Shepard vowed that his handicap would not keep him out of the big leagues once he got home. One way or another he was going to make it, of that he was sure. Welcome help soon came from fellow POW, Doug Errey, a Canadian medic who, as a civilian, had worked with amputees. Errey fashioned a crude artificial leg consisting of pieces of scrap metal, strips of leather, and rivets. The final product wasn't the fanciest looking piece of workmanship, but it did the job. Soon Bert was back on his feet and out on the recreational grounds batting, pitching, and fielding.

In February, 1945, Shepard got another big break

when a prisoner exchange brought him home. Again, he was fortunate that the transfer came at that precise moment, because little more than a month later the hospital was evacuated and the inmates required to march westward as the Soviet army approached. Safely back in the States, Bert was hospitalized in Washington, D.C.'s Walter Reed Hospital, where he was outfitted with a much better prosthesis that greatly accelerated his physical activity.

More good news lay just ahead. A few days after Bert began his rehabilitation, Assistant Secretary of War Robert Patterson dropped by to meet and chat with some of the patients. Noting Shepard's stump, he randomly asked: "What do you want to do with your life?" Without hesitating, Bert shot back: "As soon as I get a permanent leg I think I can play baseball. I want to make it to the majors."

Taken back and understandably skeptical, Secretary Patterson quickly sized up the handsome, badly injured young airman, and hurriedly concluded that Bert was the kind of fellow who could inspire and challenge other similarly disabled young men who were wounded in the war. From all appearances he was an ideal role model, who miraculously had

survived a terrible plane crash in enemy territory, lost an important limb from his body, and had endured the privations of prison life. Despite all the mishaps, Bert had not lost sight of a major goal of his life—to play baseball in the majors. Here was a man who could pump up the morale of the country's fighting forces.

With those thoughts coursing through his mind, an upbeat Patterson, who would later become Secretary of War during the Truman administration, mulled over how he could give such a well-deserving young man his break of a lifetime. After all, the St. Louis Browns had recently signed one-armed Pete Gray to a contract to play centerfield. Why not give Bert Shepard, a wounded veteran, a chance in the majors? Returning to his office, Patterson picked up the phone and called his friend Clark Griffith, owner of the American League's Washington Senators. Wasting no time with light conversation, he told Griffith that Bert was an authentic American hero, and suggested that the team owner take a look for himself. Griffith listened intently—and acted!

Shepard makes it to the majors

Less than a year after he was shot down, and little more than a month after his release from Staglag IX-C, a heady Bert Shepard strode out from a dressing room onto the baseball diamond at the University of Maryland, to try out with the Senators. A skeptical manager Ossie Bluege, whose entire major league career (1922-39) had been with the Senators, was amazed at what he saw. Here was a 25 year old banged up veteran out there running bases, snagging fly balls, fielding bunts, and sliding into base, all of it taking place in front of the rest of the team and sports writers and photographers. It was impossible—or was it!!! Bert Shepard was signed on as a playing coach for the Senators.

On July 10, Bluege tapped Shepard as the starting pitcher for the Senators against the Brooklyn Dodgers in a war relief exhibition game. Performing in front of 23,000 cheering fans, Shepard copped a 4-3 win, yielded five hits and one walk and struck out three batters. Walter Haight, a columnist for *The Sporting News* noted: "It is doubtful if any athlete in sports history has become so famous in such a short time as has Lt. Shepard."

Shepard played in his first and only official major

Bert Shepard circles bases in 1945 for Washington Senators.

league game on August 5. On that day the Senators were getting drubbed by the Boston Red Sox 14-2. In the fourth inning, Bluege motioned Bert from the bullpen. As 13,035 spectators roundly applauded and cheered him, the plucky southpaw confidently strode toward the mound.

The first batter to face him was the team's clean-up hitter, George "Catfish" Metkovich. Two men were out and the bases loaded. A sharp single by the big man could open up the floodgates even more against the embattled Senators, making their discomfort that day all the more embarrassing. One wonders what thoughts flitted through Bert's mind as he threw his warm-up pitches. Considering what he had faced over Germany, in prison, and during his recovery, "Catfish" may have looked like small potatoes as he took a few swings at the bat himself. In any case, Bert promptly struck out the slugging outfielder and retired the side. The applause from the stands was deafening.

Shepard had no problem cruising through the final four innings, allowing one run on three hits and striking out three more batters. The final score remained 14-2 in favor of the Red Sox. Despite his fine performance that day he would never make another appearance in an official major league game.

Still, Shepard would enjoy one more special moment of basking in the limelight during that epic season. On August 31, during a Senators-Yankees doubleheader, General Omar Bradley, General Jacob Devers, and Secretary Patterson presented him with the Distinguished Flying Cross and Air Medal in a touching ceremony held at home plate.

With his major league career now behind him, Shepard reenlisted in the United States Army as a captain. His primary assignment was making training films for amputees. By the time he was discharged, he had accumulated many additional honors: three Oak Leaf clusters, the Purple Heart, the European Theater Medal, a Good Conduct Award, and an Army Commendation Ribbon.

In the 1946 off season, Bert signed on to tour with a selected American League All Star team, including such baseball greats as Ted Williams and Joe DiMaggio. Many of these players had recently been discharged themselves from military service and were back on the rosters of their teams.

As player-manager at Waterbury, Connecticut, in 1949, Bert showed he could hit as well as pitch, belting four homers and stealing four bases that season. Leaving baseball for good in 1954, he moved to Hesperia, California, where he married and became a salesman and a safety engineer for the Hughes Aircraft Company. Eventually golf became his sports passion. After winning several regional tournaments, he took the national title in 1968 and 1971 at the National Amputees Golf tournament.

Still, as the years rolled along, Bert, like many other World War II veterans, never forgot the near tragic events he faced a lifetime ago. He particularly wondered what became of the courageous young doctor who saved his life. Here his story takes another remarkable turn.

In 1992 Jamie Brundell, an English businessman, during a hunting expedition in Hungary, met an Austrian physician by the name of Loidl. One evening while the two men informally exchanged personal stories, Loidl told Brundell of the role he played in saving the life of an American pilot during the war. Remembering Bert's name from his dog tags, he had often wondered what became of him.

Intrigued by the story, Brundell began to search for a "Bert Shepard" by going through American military channels. He finally located Shepard in Hesperia and passed the information along to Dr. Loidl. On Christmas Eve 1992, Bert received a special gift, a surprise telephonic holiday greeting from the man responsible for saving his life. This was too much for Bert. In May 1993 he flew to Austria where a touching reunion took place between the two men.

Down but never quite out, Bert Shepard's life had come full circle before his death on June 16, 2008, at age 87. The severe, life threatening wartime injuries very likely would have defeated a lesser man. His personal triumph over almost insurmountable odds is a powerful testimony that—with the help of a few well-timed miracles—the unattainable might just be nearer than one might think.

Oh yes, remember that memorable day back in 1945 when Bert whiffed "Catfish" Metkovich before a cheering crowd? Well, since no other similarly disabled player has ever played in the major leagues, that record quite likely will remain Shep's forever, a small town kid, who gave his best for his country, then made it to the big time for one bright, shining moment.

Chapter XII

Adrian Marks: *Daring Rescue*

Sitting at the controls of his trusty P-BY and flying only a few yards above the choppy waters of the Pacific Ocean, Navy Lieutenant Adrian Marks could hardly believe his eyes. Looking up at him were craven, despairing faces of men adrift in the unforgiving ocean. Who were they? What were they doing there? Hope for them appeared almost gone.

Only a few hours earlier that day Marks had taken off from his base at Peleiu, following receipt of a scout plane's report that over 100 men were spotted in the water 250 miles up north. He was authorized to fly up, take a look, drop supplies, and return to base. Only if the waters were calm was he permitted to land his plane. Massive 12-foot swells made it clear to Marks that the great ocean today was definitely not friendly.

As Marks continued to pass over the tragic scene, he thoughtfully considered his limited options: obey orders or disobey them and face a possible court-martial. It was that simple. Could he afford to jeopardize his peerless Navy record that pre-dated World War II? Still, here were men struggling to stay alive as they looked up to him for hope or, perhaps, even life itself.

It was Thursday, August 2, 1945. Adrian Marks of Frankfort, Indiana had come to a defining moment in his life.

Secret Mission of the USS Indianapolis

One can search the annals of United States Naval history and not find a greater tragedy than the

Lieutenant R. Adrian Marks, fourth from left, and his crew. Left to right: Richard W. Bayer, Robert G. France, Morgan F. Hensley, Donald M. Hall, Irving D. Leftkovitz, Earl R. Duxbury, Ronald A. Shepard, Max V. Ricketts (who was not on the flight), and Warren A. Kirchoff. U.S. Navy Photo.

unthinkable sinking of the heavy cruiser *USS Indianapolis (CV 35)* in the closing weeks of World War II. Commissioned on November 15, 1932 at the Philadelphia Navy Yard, the ship enjoyed a long and distinguished career abroad prior to the war. President Franklin D. Roosevelt had used the hardy vessel as his flagship during several of his "Good Neighbor" cruises to South America.

During the war, *Indianapolis* saw action in some of the hottest spots in the Pacific: Rabaul; Gilbert Islands; Marshall Islands; Tarawa; Makin; Kwajalein; Marianas Islands; Saipan; Philippine Sea; Iwo Jima; and Chichia Jima. She had a close call on March 31, 1945, when a Japanese kamikaze plane off Okinawa smashed into the port side of her after deck, killing nine men and blowing two holes in her bottom. Despite settling slightly to the stern and listing to port, the tough old girl managed to reach a salvage ship to undergo emergency repairs. Then she limped back across the Pacific to Mare Navy Yard 25 miles above San Francisco. Extensive repairs on her there made her almost as good as new.

At that precise moment the country needed a proven ship to carry out a top secret mission, so *Indianapolis* was dispatched down to Hunters Point Naval Shipyard outside San Francisco. Shortly after the ship berthed there, two trucks drove up and parked alongside her. A large crate was removed from one truck and transported to the port hanger. Two army officers removed a three-foot by four-foot lead canister from the crate, and carried it to spot near the ship commander's cabin where it was welded to the deck.

Though all of this looked a little strange to those observing the operation, no one suspected that contained inside the lead cylinder were the key elements (Uranium-235) that were necessary to arm and trigger "Little Boy," the atomic bomb that would soon fall on Hiroshima.

On July 16, 1945, *Indianapolis* headed out for Tinian in the Marianas Islands. Captured from the Japanese in August, 1944, Tinian by now was home to the busiest airfield of the war. B-29 Superfortress bombers regularly used its great runway to target Japanese sites in the Philippines, Ryukyu Islands, and even mainland Japan itself.

In command of *Indianapolis* on this fateful journey was Captain Charles McVay, a veteran officer who informed his senior officers: "I can't tell you what the mission is. I don't know myself but I've been told that every day we take off the trip is a day off the war." He bluntly added that the mysterious cylinder was considered more important than human life itself, and was to be given priority in a lifeboat ahead of any crewmember, even himself, should abandon ship become necessary.

Traveling at record speed, *Indianapolis* arrived at Tinian on July 26, delivered her unusual cargo, and was off to Guam and later her final stop at Leyte Gulf in the Philippines, presumably to participate in the expected land invasion of Japan. The ship's arrival time at Leyte was set for July 31.

Unfortunately, *Indianapolis's* good luck ran out at 11:35 p.m. on the night of Sunday, July 29, while she was proceeding on a normal course at a speed of 17 knots in moderate waters and with good visibility. Little did anyone suspect that just ahead lurked Japanese Submarine I-58, commanded by Mochitsura Hashimoto. Peering through his periscope at what appeared to be a battleship coming on fast toward him, Hashimoto saw an opportunity to strike a blow for his Emperor.

Indianapolis was 1,500 yards away when two of the sub's torpedoes blasted into the ship on her starboard (right) side forward. Crewmen who were sleeping above deck were tossed aside like rag dolls as *Indianapolis* shuddered under the heavy blows. Damage Control lost all of its water pressure. Power and communications abruptly shut down, making it impossible for the ship to send out an SOS signal. Within barely twelve minutes, the proud vessel had capsized over on her starboard side and plunged beneath the dark water, taking with her 1,199 crewmen. Grabbing hold of life preservers and whatever type of flotsam drifted by, men tried to hold on to anything available to them to survive.

It is estimated that at least 700 men survived the blast, many of whom might have been saved later had Leyte not failed to note the ship's non-arrival. How could such a fatal error occur? One limp reason given was that the "Movement Report System" never indicated that *Indianapolis* was overdue. Atmospheric interference of the ship's radio signal was also blamed for the tragic oversight.

Meanwhile, desperate men struggled to survive in the Pacific's unforgiving waters. Hundreds of them became deathly ill after ingesting sea water and oil and soon perished, along with others who sustained serious injuries from the blast. Swarms of man-eating sharks mercilessly attacked the helpless survivors.

Daring rescue at sea by Marks

Then a miracle occurred on the morning of August 2, the fourth day the men were in the water! Lieutenant Wilbur "Chuck" Gwinn, pilot of a Navy **Ventura PV-1 Bomber**, was on a routine anti-submarine patrol. As he unsuspectingly flew over the scene of horror about noon, his plane abruptly lost weight when his navigational antenna got disconnected and began flapping in the air. Turning the controls over to co-pilot Lieutenant Warren Colwell, Gwinn crawled back through the aircraft to repair the antenna. As he leaned out of the plane to guide the wire into place he spotted a long oil slick. Assuming that the slick came from an enemy vessel, Gwinn returned to the cockpit, and dropped the **Ventura** down to get a closer look. Instead, he saw the faces of delirious, ecstatic men in the ocean trying to get his attention.

Gwinn dropped an inflatable life raft and radioed back to his base at Peleiu that he had found "many men in the water" and gave his latitude and longitude. More precious time was lost, sadly, when the bureaucracy, in disbelief, failed to respond immediately to his call.

Fortunately, not everyone on Pelielu was gripped with inertia. Lieutenant Commander George Atteberry hopped aboard his plane (also a *Ventura*) to go up and take a look. Arriving at the site at 2:15 p.m. he was able to relieve Gwinn, who, by then, was running low on fuel. And more help from an unexpected source was on the way!

Also stationed on Peleiu was a handsome, mustached and quite savvy 28-year old P-BY pilot named Adrian Marks, who had flown hundreds of missions to assist and rescue downed airmen. That afternoon he carefully noted Gwinn's urgent message. An aspiring attorney prior to the war, Marks was a man of action. Wasting no time, he rounded up his 9-man crew (including himself), revved up his trusty airplane, "Playmate II," and shortly after 12:30 p.m.

was airborne. Deep in his gut he felt that something was terribly wrong up the way. Who were the men in the water? How long had they been there? How could he help if orders prohibited him from landing his plane?

PBY pilot Lieutenant R. Adrian Marks rescued 56 survivors of the U.S.S. INDIANAPOLIS. U.S. Navy Photo.

While pondering these thoughts, Marks flew over the destroyer **USS Cecil Doyle** and radioed the ship's captain, W. Graham Claytor, of Gwinn's unusual report. Going against his own orders, Claytor diverted his ship from its assigned destination at Leyte Gulf, did a 180 degree turn, and headed, instead, along the route outlined by Marks. He was 200 miles away from the site.

Reaching the disaster scene at 3:20 p.m., Marks dropped down to100 feet above the water's green surface to get a closer look. Appalled by what he saw below him, he told his crew to start tossing out rafts and supplies. Then he saw hundreds of sharks menacingly circling their prey. When the attacks began, Marks could no longer stand the scene of horror. Orders be damned, down he went to make his first and only open sea landing. "Playmate II" took two heavy blows from the heavy waves, then settled down to work its way through the great ocean swells over to a knot of survivors. Led by Ensign Morgan L. Hensley, a muscular amateur wrestler, the crew began pulling several of the men aboard. Marks was stupefied to find out that the survivors were from *Indianapolis*, the ship bearing the name of the capital of his home state. He radioed Claytor to come as fast as possible.

When the plane's interior was filled to capacity with exhausted, bone-tired, and extremely sick men, survivors were then strapped to the wings with strips of parachute shroud line to prevent them from slipping off. In all, 56 men were lifted out of the jaws of death in one of the most daring rescue missions ever made on the high seas.

As dark fell, there came additional fears and uncertainties for the men still in the water. Marks kept the *Doyle* well informed of the worsening situation. Aware that men were hanging on by the slenderest of threads and needing hope, Claytor, who would serve as Secretary of the Navy in the Carter administration, responded courageously by rushing *Doyle* along at 24 knots.

Years later Marks recalled observing the *Doyle's*

dramatic midnight arrival: "And then far out on the horizon there was a light! No matter the warning of submarines. No matter the unknown dangers of the night, the *USS Doyle* turned on her big 24 inch searchlight and pointed it straight up to reflect off the bottom of the clouds 2,000 feet up in the sky. For hour after hour it shone as a beacon of hope in the sky."

Marks, his crew, and the survivors were transferred aboard *Doyle* where they joined other men rescued by the ship. Six more rescue vessels arrived the next day along with airborne units. A thorough search was made over 100 miles of the sinking before any ship departed the tragic scene on August 8. Against all odds, 317 men of the original crew of 1,199 had survived their terrible ordeal. It was estimated that at least 200 of the men had fallen prey to sharks.

There was one final casualty: Marks requested that Captain Claytor sink "Playmate II," since it was no longer in flyable condition and might be confiscated by the Japanese. The *Doyle's* 40 mm guns blasted gaping holes in the plane and it quickly slipped beneath the ocean's surface, as Adrian Marks gave it one final salute.

Marks was never charged for his heroic rescue

Crew survivors gather on the flight deck of the escort carrier HOLLANDIA. U.S. Navy Photo.

mission. Returning home after the war, he opened a lucrative law practice in Frankfort and became a highly respected and influential community leader. Still, he never forgot the appalling events of August 2, 1945 and his role in the mighty saga. Addressing the *Indianapolis* survivors in 1975, he spoke with deep emotion: "I met you on a sparkling sun-swept afternoon of horror. I have known you through a balmy tropic night of fear. I will never forget you."

Adrian Marks died at age 81 on March 7, 1998. In the spring of 1986 I interviewed him in his rambling Frankfort home. He was one of the most eloquent, gentle, perceptive men I have ever met. Knowing him as I did over the following years, his inclusion in this book is a small effort to make sure that he, too, is never forgotten.

Lieutenant R. Adrian Marks stands beside the PBY he flew to rescue 56 men who survived the sinking of **Indianapolis**.
U.S. Navy Photo

Lieutenant "Chuck" Gwinn was the "angel" who first spotted the survivors of **Indianapolis**.
U.S. Navy Photo

*The stately **USS Indianapoli**s shown here on July 10, 1945, prior to her departure for the far pacific.*
U.S. Navy Photo

Chapter XIII

Simon Buckner: *Rebel On Okinawa*

Admiral Raymond A. Spruance, who had been a key player at Midway, was given overall command at Okinawi.

As the critical year 1945 opened, America's military forces could look back on many long, tortuous miles of island hopping across the broad Pacific Ocean. The Battle of Midway in June 1942 marked a major turning point early in the war, when Japanese forces were thrown on the defensive after their navy suffered a major reversal against a then much weaker foe. From there, the door opened for America to win notable victories at Guadalcanal, Tarawa, Saipan, Leyte Gulf, Iwo Jima, Pelilu, and many other God-forsaken places. Once Iwo Jima was fairly won, our country stood at the doorsteps of Japan herself in March 1945.

Little doubt existed among America's planners that the Empire was reeling in the wake of this inexorable march eastward. All of her Pacific island bases were gone, plucked as it were by mighty torrents of U.S. Naval firepower, daring air strikes by the Army Air Corps, and sweaty, often blood-soaked invaders sporting the ragged uniforms of the Army and Marines. Credit the Seabees for clearing out the jungles to smooth out airstrips large enough to keep America's planes within range to strike the next island. Though America had prevailed in her heady march from the disaster at Pearl Harbor, there was yet one more mountain to climb, one more island to fall.

That island was big, bustling Okinawa, a formidable piece of real estate in the Ryukyu chain, southwest of Japan and only 350 miles away. It stretched 60 miles from north to south and was 12 miles across at its largest section. A bastion of enemy strength, it boasted some 100,000 soldiers of the Japanese 32nd Army, under the command of Lieutenant-General Mitsuru Ushijimi, along with the nearby presence of a fleet still capable of inflicting deep hurt on any invading army. Okinawa offered Japan her last opportunity to escape overwhelming defeat in World War II. Japanese planners, who had not done a very good job of directing the war up to this point, hoped that Americans on the home front had grown tired of the war and would settle for a negotiated peace. Should that be the case, what happened at Okinawa might erase any possibility of a land invasion of the mainland.

Taking Okinawa was obviously crucial to America's war strategy, as well. Germany was clearly on the ropes and expected to fall most any day. That would mean a dramatic influx of battle-hardened soldiers from the European Theatre to help storm the shores of Japan. The island fortress provided excellent harbor facilities, ample land where U.S. troops could train for the expected invasion, and air bases to get the bombers and fighters into the skies. Beyond that, Okinawa would be the final jewel in America's long and costly march across the Pacific.

Aside from its strategic location and dramatic impact

One of the most famous pictures to come out of World War II is that of Marine Paul Ison charging across the battlefield toward a Japanese pill box. Just as Ison approached in full view, a TNT charge leveled the combat photographer, knocking him to the ground and sending his camera flying into the air and crashing to the ground. Fortunately, the camera was not broken and continued to take pictures, one of which was the well known one seen here.

on both sides, Okinawa would provide fodder for America's World War II veterans and buffs to discuss for years to come. For instance, the three top ranking opposing generals lost their lives near the end of the titanic struggle. These officers included Lieutenant-General Simon Bolivar Buckner, Jr., who, as head of the newly formed U.S. 10th Army, would command the land forces on Okinawa. He would also become the highest ranking American officer to die in combat during World War II. His two principal Japanese adversaries, General Ushijima, and his chief of staff, Lieutenant-General Isamu Cho, would suffer a similar fate with one difference: both of them would choose suicide to defeat.

Out of the conflict also came one of the most famous Marine photos of all time, the spirited, un-posed dash of PFC Paul "Pop" Ison across Death Valley on May 10, 1945. Ison, a 28 year old father of four, could have deferred military service but volunteered to serve in the Marines. Even today, that memorable photo is proudly displayed in Marine bases around the world; used as a recruiting tool; and depicts the highest character of those who proudly boast "Semper Fi."

Finally, and perhaps most importantly, the carnage to both sides on Okinawa convinced President Truman what step he should take to end the war before a land invasion was necessary. Truman, who had ascended to the presidency while the fight for Okinawa was going on, had seen war up close as an infantry officer during World War I. He was shaken to note that during the invasion of Iwo Jima in February, American forces had sustained more casualties than those inflicted at Normandy. In lengthy discussions with the Joint Chiefs and his military advisors, Truman's belief grew that American losses from a land invasion would be appalling.

Though the final decision on these considerations still lay ahead, time was running out on a heavy-hearted Truman who fervently hoped to find another way to end the war quickly and decisively. And there was! The yet untested atomic bomb was waiting in the wings to be used. True, the cost of taking Okinawa would be heavy, but, in the end, its outcome would lead to a thoughtful decision that would dramatically shorten the war.

What would happen on Okinawa did not escape the attention of battle-worn veterans of the battlefields across Europe. Germany collapsed to the allies on May 7, while the fight for Okinawa was nearing its peak. Men, like Oscar Masters of Patton's 3rd Army, finally could relax from the wrenching thought that tomorrow might mean another battle or skirmish. Death was always lurking just around the corner, behind the door of a shop-owner's locked up store, or concealed in heavy bush.

Masters, who had served under fire for months, finally could find some respite from battle. With his make-shift fishing pole fashioned from a jeep antenna, he located a small German stream where he landed a few trout. Yet, in the back of his mind, Masters, who was married with a small son whom he had never seen, a piercing thought remained: this war is only half over. More sprawling beaches and more heavy casualties very likely lay ahead for him. Would his luck finally run out?

General Buckner

In October 1944, the Joint Chiefs had selected Okinawa, instead of Formosa, as the launching site for the final assault on Japan. At the insistence of the War Department, the mixed force shore command would be headed by Lieutenant-General Simon Bolivar Buckner, instead of Marine General Holland "Howling Mad" Smith, who had led successful amphibious operations against the Marshalls and Saipan and Tinian in the Gilberts. At Iwo Jima he commanded Task Force 56. Along with Smith's departure from the scene, the entire team that had masterminded early successful amphibious operations was gone.

Marines go ashore on Okinawa against surprisingly light resistance.

All told, Buckner had approximately 180,000 troops serving under his command: the newly designated U.S. 10th Army included units from the 3rd Marine Division; the 1st Division; and the XIVth Army Corps. In reserve was a blending of seasoned Marine and Army boots of earlier Pacific invasions. Offering offshore support was a powerful flotilla of 1,500 warships headed by Admiral Richard Spruance, the overall commander of "Operation Iceberg," as the Okinawa operation was termed, and Vice-admiral Richmond Kelly Turner of the Fifth Fleet. Turner was the Navy's top man in amphibious warfare. It was obvious that the Americans had come to win Okinawa. No doubt about it.

A large well built man, who sported striking white hair and movie star good looks, the 58 year old General "Buck" Buckner's demeanor clearly epitomized what an army commander should be like. Still, he was well aware that he had large shoes to fill, since his father was a hero for the Confederacy during the Civil War, Lieutenant-General and later Kentucky governor, Simon Bolivar Buckner, Sr.

Buckner Jr. grew up in western Kentucky near Munfordville. He attended Virginia Military Institute prior his appointment to West Point through the assistance of President Theodore Roosevelt. Following graduation in 1908, Buckner served two tours of duty in the Philippines and experienced combat in World War I. Later, he was an instructor at West Point and the Army's General Services School at Fort Leavenworth, Kansas, prior to his appointment to the post of Executive Officer of the Army War College in Washington, D.C. Shortly before Pearl Harbor, Buckner was promoted to brigadier-general and placed in charge of the Alaskan Defense Command. Transferred to Hawaii, he organized the Tenth Army, consisting of two corps. Though he had performed well in his positions of responsibility throughout the war, Okinawa gave Buckner his first opportunity to show his wares as commander on a major combat stage.

As noted, Buckner had a decided edge against Ushijima's 100,000 defenders, augmented somewhat by the presence of a formidable air force highly trained and thoroughly indoctrinated kamikaze pilots. Knowing that his chances off turning back the invaders coming in from the north ranged from slight to nothing, Ushijima quietly withdrew his forces away from the likely invasion beaches and two strategic airfields, Kadena and Yontan. His strategy called for setting up defensive lines in the south-central portion of the island, a hilly portion of the terrain that afforded his troops better protection in huge caves and deep mountain cuts. Strong defensive lines would be thrown up around the ancient castle town of Shuri. Basically, Ushijima viewed his role as that of buying time, in order for Japan's mainland forces to better prepare their defenses once Okinawa was lost.

Ushijimi's strategy was sound in another way. By luring the Americans deeper inland, the invaders would be denied cover and support by the giant offshore fleet. Too, kamikazi pilots posed an ever-present danger to the Americans. They had already shown their prowess in earlier engagements, when Spruance, assisted by Admiral Marc Mitscher's Task Force 58, began blasting airfields on Kyushu and the Kure naval base on Honshu. In retaliation, many kamikazes slipped through Spruance's air screen on one way trips to strike several American carriers on March 19. Taking the heaviest hit that day was the 27,000 ton *Franklin*.

The *Franklin's* bold struggle to survive is one of the most heroic stories coming out of World War II. Pulverized by direct hits from two 500 pound bombs that crashed into her bridge and through the flight deck, "Big Ben" appeared headed down into the briny deep. Her cargo of 40,000 gallons of aviation fuel, incendiary bombs, and rockets began exploding, illuminating the sky and setting the sea ablaze. Captain Leslie Gehres was left with two choices; he could stay and risk the lives of those who were still able to get off the ship, or he could abandon ship and, thus, seal the fate of the men trapped below.

He chose to stay and fight to save the ship and those still alive. All able-bodied men came topside and began fighting the thick flames. Nearby ships formed a protective ring around the stricken vessel as she began an ever so tenuously departure out of the battle zone. Gradually the intrepid sailors began to regain control of their deeply wounded vessel. One boiler began operating about 9 o'clock on the first night, followed later in the evening by restoration of lights, ventilation, and communications. By noon the next day the cruiser *Pittsburg*, which had taken the carrier in tow, cast off and *Franklin* once again was dictating her own fate as she headed for repairs at Pearl Harbor. In all, 832 men perished along with 270 wounded. Approximately 550 men survived the ordeal.

"Operation Iceberg's" initial landings on Okinawa's Hagushi beaches began at 8:30 a.m., April 1, Easter Sunday. The forces came ashore at two points to form something akin to a pincer movement. Major-General Roy Geiger, Buckner's Senior Marine subordinate, led the 1st and 6th Marines at the northern end of the beaches, while the southern end was handled by Major-General John R. Hodge's 7th and 96th divisions of the XXIV Corps. From point to point, this massive amphibious assault stretched seven miles, and matched the numbers that invaded Normandy in 1944. By nightfall over 50,000 men were safely ashore.

Though the fighting would continue for 82 perilous, gut-wrenching days, the first few hours seemed like a cake-walk for veteran warriors of other Pacific invasions. With the Japanese well out of sight, Buckner's forces had no trouble overrunning the relatively quiet beaches and capturing the Kadena and Yontan airfields. Most of the men were completely baffled by the lack of resistance as they pressed inland. One soldier quipped that he had "already lived longer than I thought I would," while another fellow thought that the "Japs have quit the war." Two days later the 1st Marine Division sliced across the

A 1st Division Marine draws a bead on a Japanese sniper as his buddy ducks for cover.

Marines set off explosives in a cave near Naha to smoke out Japanese defenders inside.

southern half of Okinawa to effectively cut the island in two, well ahead of the time frame predicted by the planners of the campaign.

Such heady optimism over the initial ground success, unfortunately, soon evaporated as Ushijimi's plan began to work and the fight for Okinawa began in earnest. By the end of the first week, units of Buckner's 96th Division began smashing up against the first of three main defensive lines positioned across Kakazu Ridge, Ushijima's outermost and strongest ring of lines. As it turned out, this site proved especially troubling to the now hard-pressed Americans. For two weeks one battalion after another of the division, inched slowly up the steep incline, only to be forced to retreat under intense machine-gun and artillery fire raking their flanks both from above, and, indeed, all around them. Though momentarily thrown off balance, the gutsy Americans kept coming, determined to overrun this strategic point despite the cost. Their lines battered and partially broken, the Japanese finally withdrew down to Shuri Castle,

Ushjimi's primary line of defense.

From then on, the Americans waged almost unbroken warfare against what was described as a phantom adversary. Ushijimi's deft ruse worked this way: his men, who were mostly concealed in nearly impassable dense, thick, underbrush, would not reveal their location until their front was crossed by lead units of a platoon or company. Once the unit was in an exposed position, the Japanese would start blasting away, causing heavy casualties. Despite often fighting "blind," the Marines pressed on and took one ridge after another. Flamethrowers were used to kill and flush out Japanese soldiers hidden in the numerous caves pocketed all across the ridges.

On May 4, the embattled Ushijimi, who had served as Commandant of the Imperial Japanese Army Academy prior to coming to Okinawa, in a coordinated effort with the kamikazes decided to counterattack. It was a fatal mistake. In the initial assault, his leading elements were caught in a heavy cross-fire by their own guns. More importantly, American firepower spewed out by heavy artillery showed no quarter and easily ripped apart the attacking lines. Offshore the situation was no better, despite a few well placed hits by kamikazes on several destroyers. When the day was over, the Japanese had lost at least 6,000 men dead and numerous artillery pieces. Ushimiji would order no more counterattacks.

And so it went for several weeks in the fight for Okinawa. Casualties mounted on both sides, but Buckner's advantage steadily grew since—despite harassment by kamikazes—he could draw upon almost unlimited reserves. Ridges like Dakeshi and Wana fell. Sugarloaf Hill, with its auxiliary hills, Horseshoe and Half Moon, was taken with great cost in the face of a torrent of mortar fire, grenades, and sniper fire. A major loss there was the death of Marine Major Henry A. Courtney, Jr., who led elements of the 22nd Marines to the crest. Japanese reinforcements forced the surviving Marines to retreat on the morning of May 15. Sugar Loaf Hill held out until May 18.

This methodical slicing up of Ushimiji's exhausted

forces finally left only the Shuri Castle complex still standing. This would prove to be the biggest obstacle Buckner's weary forces would face in the entire campaign. In order to reach Shuri, it was necessary for the Americans to cross a large draw, or gully, stretching 800 yards and known as Wana Draw. Torrential rains that caused loose mud to accumulate over the draw, exacerbated the problem of getting across the area. Finding no traction on the grounds, tanks and amtracs were rendered virtually useless. Yet, despite the hazards, the intrepid Marines had caught the scent of victory and pressed on. Finally, there was good news, when aerial reconnaissance revealed on May 26 that the enemy was abandoning its Shuri defense. Shuri Castle finally belonged to the Americans.

After almost three months of heavy fighting, Buckner's 10th Army had gradually and adroitly driven Ushijima's exhausted soldiers all the way to the southern end of the island. Though the Americans continued to incur heavy losses, it was obvious that the battle was winding down.

It was at this point that Buckner, against the strong

A Corsair fighter unleashes a barrage of rocket fire on a Japanese stronghold.

advice of his staff, decided to visit a forward area to personally observe the advance of the 8th Marines. On the afternoon of June 18, he and several other officers reached an observation post occupied by units of the 2nd Marine Division. With victory at hand, the entire island would be secured within a few days, and very likely would give Buckner a major role in the approaching invasion of the Japanese mainland. It was not to be.

From the Marine outpost, Buckner could clearly see the cliffs and sandy beaches stretching across the southwestern tip of the island. Bracing himself between two large boulders about one yard apart, he lifted his binoculars to his eyes to survey the landscape. As far as he could tell, everything in the general vicinity appeared safe and secure. But not quite! In the distance a spotter for the Japanese 1st Artillery saw what appeared to be a group of high ranking American officers silhouetted against some large boulders. Carefully studying their movements, he thought he could he get off a lethal artillery shot.

Satisfied that the situation was under control, Buckner placed his binoculars back in the case, snapped it shut, and prepared to leave. At that moment the Japanese officer gave the order to fire. Five artillery rounds landed on the tempting target. One shell struck a boulder, showering chips, shrapnel, and coral fragments in all directions, some of which dug into Buckner's chest and abdomen. Heavy bleeding could not be stanched and within 10 minutes he was dead. Amazingly, the blast did not kill or injure any other members of the party.

Ushijima's and Cho's exits into eternity on June 21 were in marked contrast to that of Buckner. Their last headquarters cave (inside Hill 89 to the Americans) was only approximately one mile from where Buckner met his untimely fate. Clad in his full dress uniform, Ushijima called his junior officers together and exhorted them to fight to the end for the Emperor. Cho was attired in a white ceremonial kimono for the occasion. After toasting themselves and their staff with scotch whiskey, the two men stepped outside onto a narrow ledge overlooking the ocean 200 feet below. Kneeling on a white cloth, Ushijima lifted a knife, opened his tunic, and, with a loud shout, drove the blade into his stomach. Moments later Cho followed his lead. Once the burial ceremony was over, several of the Japanese officers reportedly blew out their brains.

With the enemy's major officer staff opting for eternity as opposed to fighting, it is little wonder that Okinawa quickly fell to the victorious Americans a few days later. Called the "Typhoon of Steel," the costly operation resulted in U.S. forces sustaining approximately 12,513 dead or missing and 38,916 wounded. Japanese casualties topped 66,000 dead or missing and 17,000 wounded. Only 7,455 Nipponese soldiers were captured. Including 80,000 civilians, the casualties totaled approximately 200,000 lives.

Offshore, U.S. Navy casualties were also quite high due to the relentless (and senseless) enemy kamikaze assaults made against the ships. Close to 5,000 sailors died and 5,000 more were wounded by the attacks.

No question about it, America had notched another overwhelming victory. The loss of Okinawa left Japanese planners with a heavily decimated army, along with the loss of hundreds of aircraft and their huge 78,800 ton battleship *Yamoto*, once Admiral Yamamoto's flagship and the pride of the Japanese fleet. Despite all these heady achievements, only a few of the American victors could exalt over the outcome.

So, what was the rub? Simply stated, the victors knew that though Okinawa was theirs, there yet remained the stark reality that a land invasion was necessary to bring down the Empire once and for all. The gallant men who had fought so tenaciously to prevail at Okinawa would, very likely, be at the forefront of the assault. The enemy, resolute and fanatical, would give no quarter in the defense of his homeland. A blood bath lay ahead. How could anyone rest upon their laurels despite taking Okinawa. As Ronald Spector posed in his notable book *Eagle Against The Sun*: "If the capture of a base (Okinawa) in the Ryukus had been this bad, what would the assault on Japan itself be like?"

Fortunately, that day never came. At that moment an atomic bomb was finally being secretly tested to determine its effectiveness in warfare. President Truman now knew that the time had come to end the bloody mess Japan had imposed on America four years earlier. There would not be another body strewn beach filled with young Americans. While he was at the Potsdam Conference (July 17-August 2), the President was notified of the successful test of an atomic bomb in Nevada. Wasting no time, he bluntly warned Japan: "Immediate, unconditional surrender or suffer utter devastation." The Empire said "No." The die was now irrevocably cast. Truman passed a note to Secretary of War Henry Stimson: "Release when ready."

On August 6 the powerful B-29 *Enola Gay* rose into the heavens on its way to drop the world's first atomic bomb on Hiroshima. A few days later a second one fell from the bomb bay doors of *Bock's Car.* Japan capitulated a few days later and the most deadly war in human history finally was over. The heavy price paid by American forces at Okinawa was not in vain.

First interred in the 10th Army Cemetery on Okinawa, Buckner's remains were later returned to Frankfort, Kentucky, the state capitol, for burial next to his father's grave.

He is remembered today at several places: a small memorial on Okinawa at a site named Fort Buckner; Camp Buckner at West Point, where sophomores get their first taste of Army life outside the classroom; and Buckner Gymnasium at Fort Richardson, Anchorage, Alaska, a post he established during his assignment there.

There are several interesting footnotes to the victory at Okinawa. Once Shuri Castle fell, Captain Julius Dusenberg of the 5th Marine Regiment took off his helmet, and removed a Confederate battle flag he had carried in honor of Buckner as the son of a Confederate leader. Fashioning a simple flag pole from a bruised tree sapling, he raised the flag to the highest point of Shuri Castle. Thus, the Confederate battle flag was displayed on Okinawa before the Star and Stripes went up high atop Hill 89 on June 29, attesting that the battle was officially over.

What became of Oscar Masters, the young fellow who dipped his fishing pole into a meandering German stream and wondered, as did many other survivors of European battlefields, what lay ahead for him. Today, at a young 91 years, he is a retired successful businessman living in Greenville, South Carolina. Still active in church and community groups, he frequently speaks to local organizations about his experiences in World War II. A loyal patriot, Masters

has made two trips to Washington's World War II Memorial and actively encourages other veterans to do likewise.

Marine Paul "Pop" Ison survived his 75 yard charge across Death Valley's open ground, and came home to his wife and four children in Fort Myers, Florida. In later years as the famous photo made its rounds he became an iconic figure. His full head of white hair and courtly manner endeared him to both young Marines and the top brass of the Marine Corps. Pop passed away on October 3, 2001, still boasting of himself as one of the proud and the few. His name today is preserved by members of the Fort Myers Chapter of the Marine Corps League, who named their group, "Paul Ison Chapter."

To be sure, Okinawa was a long and costly operation. America's decisive victory there was bought with a terrible cost. Yet, by paying such a price the men who fell on Okinawa brought what appeared to be a distant victory over Japan, much nearer than any planner anticipated when "Operation Iceberg" kicked off that Easter Sunday. Hundreds of thousands of American youth would come home to live out their lives as a result of Okinawa.

Oscar Masters

93

*America's great victory at Okinawa, followed by the two atomic missions, hastened the end of the war. On September 2, 1945, General Douglas McArthur, seated, signed the surrender papers with Japan on board **the USS Missouri.** U.S. Navy Photo.*

Chapter XIV

Paul Tibbets: *Hiroshima*

The crew of the ENOLA GAY. Front row, left to right: Caron, Stoborik, Duzenburg, Nelson, and Shumard. Back row: Ferebee, Van Kirk, Tibbets, and Lewis. U.S. Army Photo.

By the summer of 1945 America had reached a critical point in the war against Japan. Having gotten up off the mat after Pearl Harbor, the country's military forces had marched inexorably across the Pacific almost to the shores of the Empire itself. Island after island had fallen as our country's armed forces gave blood, sweat, and tears to take the fight directly to the enemy.

Then came the invasion of Okinawa, a giant island only 340 miles from mainland Japan. Called the "Typhoon of Steel," the costly operation fought there from March 18 to June 23, 1945, resulted in huge casualties on both sides: United States forces sustained approximately 12,513 dead or missing and 38,916 wounded, while Japanese casualties topped 66,000 dead or missing and 17,000 wounded.

Offshore, Navy losses were also quite high due to the relentless (and senseless) enemy kamikaze assaults against our ships. Approximately 5,000 sailors died and 5,000 more were wounded by the needless attacks. Civilian casualties numbered as many as 80,000 people killed or wounded.

Though taking Okinawa gave America another clear victory in the Pacific, the heavy losses incurred there cast a pale over what our country should do next. As Ronald Spector posed in his book **EAGLE AGAINST THE SUN**: "If the capture of a base (Okinawa) in the Ryukus had been this bad, what would the assault on Japan itself be like?" Fortunately, at that critical moment America was on the verge of producing a powerful secret weapon, an atomic bomb. The use of that weapon from the bomb bay of a B-29 would bring Japan to her knees within weeks. One airplane in particular, the ***Enola Gay***, and her pilot, Paul Tibbets, would play the key roles in the final outcome in the skies over Japan.

To understand what was at stake, one must go back to 1939 when Germany began secretive work on an atomic bomb. Though aware of what Germany was up to, an isolationist United States did nothing until August 1942, when the top secret "Manhattan Project" began under the auspices of the Army Corps of Engineers. It was directed by the tough-minded, no non-sense General Leslie R. Groves, who had only recently supervised the construction of the Pentagon outside Washington, D.C. With his facilities strategically located in Oak Ridge, Tennessee; Eastern Washington State; and Los Alamos, New Mexico, Groves, incredibly, guided the project through basic research production of fissile material and testing within three years. As 1945 opened, "Manhattan" was at the threshold of producing the world's first atomic bomb.

President Truman's options to end the war

In November 1944, President Franklin Roosevelt was reelected to a fourth term, and selected Missouri Senator, Harry S. Truman as his vice-presidential running mate. Roosevelt, of course, knew of the bomb's progress from its inception but Truman was completely unaware of the project at the time of the election.

That changed when Roosevelt died of a fatal cerebral hemorrhage and Truman assumed the presidency on April 12, 1945. Following the brief White House swearing-in ceremony, Truman called a Cabinet meeting. As the brief session was breaking up, Secretary of War Henry L. Stimson casually took Truman off to the side to inform him that very soon, within weeks possibly, the United States would have a weapon of extraordinary destructive power that could end the war earlier than expected. Truman listened intently but could not comprehend exactly what Stimson was talking about. Twelve days later Stimson and Groves thoroughly briefed the new President at the White House on the still untested bomb.

Germany's collapse ended the war in Europe on May 9, V-E Day. A greatly relieved Truman knew that though one war was over, another one was still raging in the Pacific. In a somber note to his mother he wrote: "We have another war to win and people must realize it. I hope they will, anyway." As an infantry officer during World War I, Truman had seen the ugly face of war up close. He was not naïve when tallying up the cost in American casualties should an invasion of the Japanese mainland become necessary.

Japan's military forces, for instance, could still pit 2.3 million troops against an invading army, including 10,000 aircraft, many of them manned by the infamous "kamikaze" suicide pilots. Suicide boats and human torpedoes would defend the beaches. Local militia and ordinary citizens were also expected to take up the fight even if it meant strapping explosives to their bodies. Under its harsh military rule, Japan was obviously preparing to commit national suicide in a desperate effort to ward off inevitable defeat.

Though Japan's fate had been sealed once the Marianas Islands fell in 1944, our own military planners had to carefully consider the heavy cost to America of a land invasion. Some estimates placed the loss in life alone as high as 500,000 Americans. Back home even ordinary citizens knew quite well the cost paid by those men who had assaulted the beaches at Normandy, and subsequently marched across France, Belgium, and into Germany. Could the men who fought in the Hurtgen Forest, held on at the Bulge, and pushed up the Italian Peninsula be called upon one last time to shed their blood to bring down Japan?

Aware of all this, there was emerging a faint mummer in some quarters that America should settle for a negotiated peace. Japan knew this and was preparing to go for broke as the invasion loomed on the horizon.

During the Potsdam Conference (July 17 to August 2, 1945), Truman was notified of the successful test of an atomic bomb at Alamogordo, New Mexico. Having carefully weighed his options prior to receiving this critical information, the new President had no trouble reaching a decision: he would drop the bomb and end the ghastly war. Knowing he held the trump card, he bluntly warned Japan to surrender unconditionally and immediately in order to avoid "utter destruction." Still unaware of the existence of an atomic bomb, Japan, not surprisingly, responded negatively. The die was now cast from which there would be no turning back. On July 30 Truman sent Stimson a handwritten note: "Release when ready."

Paul Tibbets and the 509th Composite Group

The unit that was responsible for delivering the atomic bomb was known as the 509th Composite Group, an elite group of airmen handpicked by a 29-year old lieutenant-colonel named Paul W. Tibbets, Jr. The son of Paul Warfield and Enola Gay Tibbets, he was born on February 23, 1915, in Quincy, Illinois. The family moved to Florida when he was nine. Three years later at an air show, a barnstorming pilot named Doug Davis took the youngster up in a Waco 9 airplane, an experience that fixated Tibbets on flying. His high school years were spent at Western Military Academy, where he met another future World War II pilot, Ed "Butch" O'Hare. From there he enrolled at the University of Florida, later transferring to the University of Cincinnati to pursue a degree in medicine, in compliance with his parent's wishes. Still, flying was his first love, so he dropped out of college and joined the Army Air Corps in 1937.

A born leader, Tibbets advanced up the ranks while stationed at Fort Benning, Georgia. He piloted the A-20, the army's latest attack bomber; the B-18 on patrols; and transferred to the B-17 *Flying Fortress* as commander of the 97th Bomb Group shortly after Pearl Harbor.

On August 17, 1942, flying out of the American air base near Polebrook, England, Tibbets led 18 "Forts" on the first American daylight bombing raid over German-occupied Europe, striking Rouen and Buddicum. Later that year he flew General Mark Clark to a secret meeting in Algiers. Topping the list was his selection by General Eisenhower to pilot the Supreme Commander to critical meetings with allies

Her mission completed, the ENOLA GAY heads for a safe landing back at Tinian. U.S. Army Photo.

or field officers.

In July 1943 Tibbets arrived in Wichita, Kansas, where he was introduced to the Boeing B-29 bomber, a technological marvel at that time. Appropriately called the **Superfortress**, the B-29 was not every pilot's dream but it certainly was ideally suited for Tibbets. It had four 2,000 horsepower engines; boasted a maximum speed of 360 miles per hour; could climb up to 33,600 feet; and travel 3,250 miles without refueling. Tibbets was placed in charge of flight testing the powerful new bomber that one day would spearhead the great bombing missions over the Japanese mainland.

On September 1, 1944, Tibbets was ordered to Colorado Springs, Colorado, where he met with Major-General Uzal G. Ent, commanding general of the Second Air Force. Also present at the highly secret meeting were Dr. Norman Ramsey, a 29-year old Harvard physicist; Navy Captain William "Deke" Parsons, a member of the Manhattan Project and explosives expert; and Colonel John Lansdale, an Army Intelligence Officer.

Once the brief formalities were out of the way, Ramsey bluntly asked Tibbets if he had ever heard of atomic energy. Tibbets responded that having majored in physics he knew the atomic scale. Next Parsons inquired if he was aware of any present activity going on in the field of developing atomic energy. Tibetts said he understood German scientists were actively working to find a way to split the atom. Ramsey interjected that the United States was already beyond that stage and was now concentrating on developing a powerful bomb with a force of 20,000 tons of conventional high explosives. Once the bomb was ready to use, airplanes would be needed to deliver and drop the bomb(s) at designated places on both Germany and Japan. This give and take continued for an hour or so, then everyone left the room with the exception of General Ent and Tibbets.

Ent, who had headed the successful 1943 bombing raids on the Polesti (Romanian) Oil Fields, quickly got to the point, telling Tibbets that General "Hap" Arnold, commander of the Army Air Corps, had suggested three men, including Tibbets, to head a top secret assignment directly connected to delivering atomic bombs. Two of the officers were full colonels while Tibbets was a lieutenant-colonel. No problem,

since Tibbets was considered the much better qualified man for the job. Ent went on to outline the vast authority that Tibbets would wield in this position. For instance, by merely mentioning the code word "Silverplate" he could have virtually anything he requested. Concluding, Ent sounded an ominous note: "Paul, if you're successful you'll probably be called a hero. And if you fail, you might wind up in prison."

Tibbets wasted no time pulling together a crack organization. Consisting of pilots, navigators, engineers, and mechanics, the men who comprised the 509th began their B-29 training on December 17, 1944, in Wendover, Utah, the remote training site personally selected by Tibbets. In May 1945 the 509th left dusty Wendover for Tinian in the Marianas Islands. Within three months, the work of this dedicated group of young Americans would bring the Japanese Empire crashing down.

When the Japanese did not reply to Truman's dire warning of July 30, preparations were sped up to drop the first atomic bomb. General Curtis Lemay, who

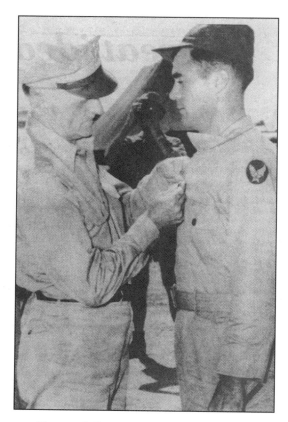

General Spaatz awards Tibbets the
Distinguished Service Cross.

was leading the successful conventional bombing attacks over Japanese cities, selected Hiroshima for the first mission because of its strategic location in southwestern Honshu Island; its numerous war factories; and its headquarters of the 43,000 man Japanese Second Army. Tibbets named himself pilot of the B-29 selected for the mission. Known simply as *No. 82*, the airplane was renamed by Tibbets *Enola Gay* after his mother's maiden name.

Crew members included Captain Robert A. Lewis, co-pilot; Major Thomas W. Ferebee, bombardier; Captain Theodore J. Van Kirk, navigator; Staff Sergeant Wyatt E. Duzenbury, flight engineer; Sergeant Robert H. Shumard, assistant flight engineer; Private First Class Richard H. Nelson, radio operator; Staff Sergeant George R. Caron, tail gunner; and Sergeant Joseph S. Stiborik, radar operator. Three mission specialists were added to the group: the aforementioned Navy Captain William "Deak" Parsons, weaponeer and ordnance officer; Lieutenant Jacob Beser, radar countermeasures officer; and Lieutenant Morris R. Jepperson, assistant weaponeer.

The bomb that was loaded onto the giant airplane was called "Little Boy." Struck by its size and weight, Tibbets thought it was a "monster compared with any bomb that I had ever dropped. 'Little Boy' was 28 inches in diameter and 12 feet long. Its weight was more than 9,000 pounds. With its coat of dull gunmetal paint, it was an ugly monster."

Special Bombing Mission No. 13

At 2:30 a.m. on Sunday, August 6, Paul Tibbets gunned the *Enola Gay's* powerful motors and taxied to Tinian's southwest end of North Field runway to prepare for takeoff. With 7,000 gallons of gasoline and a 9,000 pound bomb on board, the powerful airplane trembled and shook during the engine's warm-up.

Cleared for takeoff at 2:15 a.m., Tibbets began his long run toward the sea almost two miles away, lifting off at 155 mph near the end of the runway. Special Bombing Mission No. 13 was underway. Five other B-29s flew along with the *Enola Gay* that morning. Three weather scout airplanes led the way, while trailing behind were *The Great Artiste* and *No. 91*. Still, it was a lonely mission for the *Enola Gay*; only she would drop the bomb and only she would

The ENOLA GAY forms the backdrop at Roswell, New Mexico, for Colonel Tibbets, bombardier Tom Ferebee, and the base commander (unidentified). U.S. Army Photo.

99

suffer catastrophic consequences should something go awry.

At 6:30 a.m. Parsons dropped down into the cramped space of the bomb bay, removed three green plugs from the bomb's casing and attached three red plugs. "Little Boy" was now activated and ready to go. Once that procedure was out of the way, Tibbets spoke over the intercom to his crew: "We are carrying the world's first atomic bomb. When the bomb is dropped, Lieutenant Beser will record our reactions. This recording is for history, so watch your language."

Shortly after 8 a.m. the city of Hiroshima came into view, the morning sunlight glistening off its tall buildings. The surrounding landscape that unfolded before the crew was exactly what aerial photographs had indicated. The only thing left to do was locate the I.P. (Initial Point) on which the bomb was to be aimed. Bombardier Tom Ferebee, described by Tibbets as the "best bombardier who ever looked through the eyepiece of a Norden bombsite," was the first to spot the drop point about 10 miles away. It was the T-shaped Atoi bridge that stood in the center of the unsuspecting city of 300,000 people.

At 8:15 a.m. Hiroshima time (Monday) Ferebee shouted "Bomb Away." The bomb-bay door snapped open and "Little Boy" sprang free from its harness to plummet toward the earth. Japan's fate was irrevocably sealed. With the sudden release of almost 10,000 pounds of extra weight, the *Enola Gay* lurched upward. Now it was time to clear out and head home. In conventional bombing the pilot flew straight ahead once the explosives were released. An atomic blast on the ground, however, required a special maneuver by the pilot to put as much distance as possible between his airplane and the explosion. In order to escape from a likely disaster, it was necessary for the pilot to turn the aircraft around and quickly fly away from the site of the explosion. Tibbets had practiced this maneuver numerous times and on this day, with clock-like precision, he swung the *Enola Gay* around in a diving right hand turn of 155 degrees.

Elbert Watson, center, with two authentic American heroes of World War II: Paul Tibbets and George Gay.
Author's Collection.

Down on the ground air raid sirens began wailing as the city reacted to the approaching airplanes, though suspecting nothing of what was coming at them. Forty-three seconds later "Little Boy" exploded within 800 feet of the Atoi Bridge, bringing on the Atomic Age in a dramatic and deadly fashion. Though Tibbets. was already over 11 miles away, the *Enola Gay* was pummeled by the tremendous blast. A giant upward flash lighted up the airplane's instrument panels and caused a brilliant glare. Next came a sharp acceleration that resembled a huge gray ball of compressed air that bounced the crew members around inside the aircraft like rag dolls. Once a second blow had passed through the airplane everything quickly settled down. Her dramatic mission over, things settled down and the *Enola Gay* almost serenely continued her long odyssey home and into history.

After spending twelve hours and thirteen minutes in the air, the hardy airplane touched down on Tinian at 2:58 p.m. An enthusiastic crowd of over 200 officers and enlisted men turned out to greet the crew. Included in the group was General Carl "Tooey" Spaatz, commander of the Strategic Air Force in the Pacific, and General Nathan Twining, commander of the 20th Air Force in the Marianas. Spaatz, who had authorized both the conventional and atomic bombing strikes against Japan, had flown over from his headquarters in Guam to personally award Tibbets the Distinguished Service Cross.

Meanwhile, Truman, who was on his way back to Washington from Potsdam, did not mince words: "It is an atomic bomb. . . It was to spare the Japanese people from utter destruction that the ultimatum of July 20 was issued at Potsdam. Their leaders promptly rejected that ultimatum. If they do not now accept our terms they may expect a rain of ruin from the air, the like of which has never been seen on this earth." Fortunately, reason finally emerged from among Japan's military leaders several days later, but only after a second bomb leveled Nagasaki, finally ending the war abruptly and decisively.

While assigned to the Pentagon in 1948, Tibbets was invited to the White House to meet President Truman for the first and only time in his life. Also present at the meeting were Spaatz, General Jimmy Doolittle, and Colonel David Shilling, a World War II air ace. Upon entering the Oval Office, a relaxed, beaming Truman walked over to each man and congratulated him for his service to the country. When he came to Tibbets he paused a few moments then queried, "What do you think?" Tibbets responded that he carried out the Hiroshima mission as instructed. Truman slapped his hand down on the desk and said: "You're damn right you did, and I'm the guy who sent you. If anybody ever gives you a hard time about it, send them to me."

Paul Tibbets went on to become a brigadier-general. In 1946 he served as a technical adviser in the Bikini Atom Bomb Tests. He later played a key role in establishing the National Military Command Center in the Pentagon. After 30 years of distinguished military service, he retired from the Air Force in 1966. He is enshrined with honor in the National Aviation Hall of Fame at Wright-Patterson AFB in Dayton, Ohio. In addition to the Distinguished Service Cross, his other military awards included the Legion of Merit, Distinguished Flying Cross, Purple Heart, Air Medal, Commendation Medal, European-African-Middle Eastern Campaign Medal, Asiatic-Pacific Campaign Medal, American Defense Service Medal, American Campaign Medal, and World War II Victory Medal.

Often regarded as the one man most responsible for ending World War II, General Tibbets passed away on November 1, 2007, in his Columbus, Ohio home. To the end of his life he never regretted the crucial role he played in developing the organization responsible for effectively delivering the atomic bomb, or his part in carrying out the Hiroshima mission. Often remarking that during war people—many of them innocent bystanders—always get killed, he confessed that he had never lost a minute's sleep over his part in ending the war.

As for the *Enola Gay*, the historic aircraft was eventually completely restored by the Smithsonian's National Air and Space Museum, and placed on permanent display in 2003 at the Steven F. Udvar-Hazy Center near Dulles International Airport outside of Washington, D.C.

*Following his historic mission, Tibbets poses alongside the **Enola Gay**. Author's collection.*

Chapter XV

Chuck Sweeney: *Final Mission*

"Chuck" Sweeney poses in front of BOCK'S CAR on Tinian shortly after his successful mission over Nagasaki. U.S. Army Photo.

Major Charles "Chuck" Sweeney squirmed around in the cockpit as he impatiently awaited takeoff in **Bockscar**, the B-29 that would take him on a critical bombing mission to Kokura, Japan, and into the history books. Unanticipated problems had already delayed his departure from Tinian's Runway A, one of the island's massive macadamized airstrips.

Only 25 years of age, Sweeney was heading a seasoned crew who were totally dedicated to their work. In the hours ahead each man would prove his mettle under the most trying circumstances imaginable.

Bockscar was one of the 15 "Silverplate" B-29s assigned to the 393rd Bombardment Squadron of the 509th Composite Group stationed on Tinian. Built at the Martin Aircraft Plant (now Offutt Air Force Base) at Omaha, Nebraska, for approximately $500,000, the sleek airplane was flown by Captain Frederick C. Bock from Wendover Army Air Field, Utah, to Tinian in early June, 1945.

Normally, Sweeney would have flown the *Great Artist*, the plane he had piloted on the August 6 Hiroshima mission as the blast measurement aircraft.

Besides manning a crew and piloting an expensive airplane, Sweeney knew that another important commodity was on board, a bomb the likes of which he had never seen before. Dubbed "Fat Man" (probably named after Prime Minister Winston Churchill), it was the second atomic bomb that would be dropped on Japan within three days.

Fastened securely in the bomb bay, "Fat Man" presented an interesting contrast to its older brother "Little Boy," the atomic bomb dropped on Hiroshima. Weighing 10,300 pounds (1,000 pounds more than "Little Boy"), it was 10 feet eight inches long and five feet across. Painted with high gloss yellow enamel replete with black tail fins, Sweeney thought it resembled "a grossly oversized decorative squash." Its cost was somewhere in the neighborhood of two billion dollars.

Sweeney's work this day was definitely cut out for him. Normally, he would have flown *The Great Artiste*, the blast measurement aircraft he had piloted on the Hiroshima mission. Inclement weather predicted for much of Japan on the day of the scheduled mission, however, caused the time of the second mission to be moved up to today, August 9. Since the Hiroshima instrumentation had not been removed from *Great Artiste*, Sweeney traded airplanes and crew with that of *Bockscar.*

Despite his youth, Sweeney was no novice when it came to airplanes and flying. In fact, his youthful appearance belied a tough, tenacious no-nonsense fellow who was known for giving his best to any duty assigned to him.

Born in Lowell, Massachusetts, on December 27, 1919, he was instilled with a strong sense of patriotism by his Catholic parents who revered President Roosevelt. After graduating from Quincy (Massachusetts) High School, he attended Boston University and Purdue University (West Lafayette, Indiana). Joining the Army Air Corps on April 28, 1941 as an aviation cadet, he received his pilot's commission and lieutenant's wings the following December.

Sweeney's first assignment was at Jefferson Proving Grounds, a 100 square mile military reservation near Madison, Indiana, on the Ohio River. There he was introduced to a whole new world of naked firepower. Conventional iron bombs, rockets, fire bombs, and howitzer shells were all fired daily from big guns or dropped from aircraft. One of two test pilots attached to Jefferson, Sweeney was able to pick up flight time in the more advanced aircraft available at that time, among them B-24s, B-25s, A-20 bombers, and P-47 fighters. Flight testing, he found, was designed to demonstrate that ordnance coming directly off the production line "would perform as intended, detonate when expected, and produce the blast yield within specification."

Though at that time he had no idea what all this might lead to, this training would bode well for him as he sat at the controls of *Bockscar* that morning chomping at the bits to get the airplane in the air.

After spending 18 months at Jefferson and gaining a promotion to captain, the 23-year old Sweeney was reassigned to Eglin Field in the Florida panhandle. Serving there as both an operations officer and test pilot, he was given command of the main field and nine surrounding auxiliary fields; all of the aircraft not having a specific function; and a large operational staff—not a bad start for a young officer definitely on the way up.

Better things lay just ahead! Call it luck, fate, or Divine Intervention, Sweeney was about to meet a man and be introduced to an airplane that, together, would change his life forever and immortalize his name in America's history books.

In September 1943, Sweeney was informed by Eglin's commanding officer's aide that a B-29 airplane would arrive that afternoon from Seattle. His job was to assign extra military police to Hanger 17; cordon off the area; and make sure unauthorized personnel did not get within 300 feet of the airplane. Sweeney thought he knew everything the military was putting in the skies at that time, but a B-29–what was that?

His curiosity thoroughly aroused, Sweeney arrived early at the control tower to get a good look at the mysterious airplane when it arrived. In the distance he finally saw a small silver dot that slowly grew into the largest airplane he had ever seen. He could not take his eyes off the massive, beautiful bird as it gracefully descended toward the field.

Dashing down from the tower he confiscated a jeep and sped over to the landing strip, where he stared in awe at the aircraft as it taxied to a stop only a few feet from him. As he studied the features of the airplane, Lieutenant-Colonel Paul Tibbets, the pilot, exited from beneath the airplane's forward compartment. Attired in a perfectly fitted flying suit, the handsome Tibbets impressed Sweeney as quite a special fellow to command such an amazing machine. He must get to know him and find out what was going on.

The hoped for meeting came sooner than Sweeney expected. That night at the Officer's Club he spotted Tibbets enter the room alone. He quickly arose and invited him over to his table for dinner. That night Sweeney got a crash course in the nuts and bolts of the B-29. Though somewhat guarded in his remarks, Tibbets said he brought the airplane to Eglin to run it through some special tests involving the central fire control system. Rather casually he hinted that he needed extra pilots to fly target tow for the planes.

Seeing his opening, Sweeney blurted out that he would love to join Tibbets's outfit. He knew there would be special requirements but he was confident of his ability to fly. Matter-of-factly, Tibbets replied: "That may be a possibility." Obviously impressed with the young officer, Tibbets used him as his co-pilot a few weeks later on a couple of flights, once on a hop out to Wichita in a B-26. On the return flight, Tibbets selected a B-29 and permitted Sweeney to get the feel of the plane by sharing the cockpit with him.

When two more B-29s arrived at Eglin, Tibbets offered Sweeney the opportunity to take one of them up to test fire the system. Settling into the pilot's seat the next morning, Sweeney pushed the stick forward, pointed the airplane down the runway, and prepared for take-off in what he described as a "technological marvel." Both the take-off and 20 hour test firing flight were flawless, as was his near picture perfect touchdown. From that moment on the B-29 was Sweeney's airplane. Perhaps more importantly he was now officially one of Tibbets's boys.

Promoted to the rank of major, Sweeney was briefly assigned to Grand Island, Nebraska, where he instructed the crusty old cigar chomping general, Curtis LeMay, the commander of the 20th Air Force, in the operations of the B-29. Stationed in the Marianas Islands, the 20th was presently preparing for its massive fire-bombing missions over Japan. Since the B-29 was the plane he would use, LeMay expected nothing short of perfection in obtaining information about all facets of its operation. Sweeney proved a capable instructor.

On September 11 Sweeney arrived at Wendover Field, Utah, a desolate, primitive sort of installation that was boxed in by the Great Salt Lake on one side and an endless expanse of desert on the other. Miles of barren salt flats surrounded the isolated base. The nearest town only boasted a population of 103 people. Especially selected by Tibbets, Wendover would prove to be the ideal spot to train the men who would drop the atomic bombs on Japan.

At this point Sweeney had little idea what this was leading up to and the role he might play in the coming events. One day some of his questions were answered when Captain Meade McClanahan drove him out into the desert. After traveling several miles, McClanahan stopped the car and both men got out and walked a short distance. McClanahan stooped down and picked up a handful of dirt. Looking Sweeney directly in the eye, he said America's scientists were working on a new weapon expected to be 20,000 times more powerful than any existing bomb. He abruptly threw the dirt into the air, remarking: "One bomb will reduce an entire city to this." For Sweeney, it was a somber, gut-wrenching crash course in Advanced Physics, or, more precisely, Einstein's theory of relativity i.e. that unlimited quantities of pure energy could be generated into tiny particles of matter. He wondered if he would be called upon to drop such a weapon one day.

The next day Tibbets got with Sweeney in an isolated, virtually barren building at the far end of Wendover Field. Only a security guard was present for the meeting. Tibbets quietly explained that his duty was to create a composite group that would function outside the usual military command. Almost entirely self-supporting, this organization would be supported by its "own bomber, transport, military police, material, ordnance, engineering, air service, and base service squadrons." Sweeney could not believe his ears: he was serving under a lieutenant-colonel whose power extended well beyond that given most generals.

Men began to arrive at Wendover to serve in the special project. None were more important than the members of the 393rd Bombardment Squadron, a crack unit that was eagerly anticipating its deployment to Europe. To get this bunch, all Tibbets had to do was utter the magic word "Silverplate" and, presto, he had them!

Still, Tibbets clearly understood the importance of maintaining unit morale. Though Sweeney was his pick to head this crack unit, he knew that the group was commanded by Lieutenant-Colonel Thomas J. Classen, a competent and well-respected officer. To resolve the dilemma he named Sweeney deputy commander of the 393rd, and a few weeks later kicked Classen upstairs to the position of deputy commanding officer of the 509th Composite Group, as the group was now known. Sweeney then assumed complete command of the 393rd.

Approximately 1500 men eventually arrived at Wendover. Most of them hated the place with unrequited passion. Its unforgiving heat, remote location, primitive living standards, dank drinking water, and the ever-present dust that clogged their nostrils, convinced many of the men that they had, indeed, passed through the Gates of Hell itself. Despite the adverse conditions, they sensed that they were the best or they would not be in this God-forsaken place! Something big was going on and they were part of it.

Tibbets obviously saw a much larger picture. Tinian, a small island in the Marianas chain and only 1300 miles from Japan, had fallen to American forces in

June 1944. Several thousand Seabees constructed airfields large enough to accommodate any heavy bomber. Aware that Tinian was within easy reach of the B-29s, Tibbets visited the island in early 1945 to personally assess the island's capability for use as an airbase from which the 509th could operate. Once he was satisfied, the stage was set for D-Day over Japan.

In June 1945 the 509th left Wendover and headed for Tinian. To their surprise, they found the entire island transformed into what resembled a huge airport. Since Tinian was shaped similarly to New York City's Manhattan Island, the men who laid out the place decided to copy the "Big Apple's" design—within certain limits, of course. A Broadway, 42nd Street, Eighth Avenue, and Lennox Avenue were created, and a touch of Brooklyn was thrown in for the Flatbush Gang that showed up. Though the place didn't exactly convey the feeling of home for the men, its two giant Seabee constructed airstrips dwarfed anything they had seen previously.

Sweeney's perilous mission

All of that was history to Sweeney. What mattered now was that less than two years after he first climbed into the pilot's seat of a B-29, he was about to undertake a mission that possibly would alter the course of the war and forever change the course of history. The climb to the top had been nothing short of miraculous for the young son of a Catholic workingman's family

Very likely none of that was on Sweeney's mind as he impatiently awaited takeoff. Just then the first of many problems cropped up that would plague the mission to no end. To his dismay, flight engineer John Kuharek discovered that 600 gallons of fuel was trapped and not pumping. This left *Bockscar* with only 6,400 gallons instead of the 7,000 considered necessary to reach Japan and return to Tinian. Still, it was possible for the plane to carry out its mission if everything else went off without a hitch.

Since it was too late to correct the fuel intake problem or transfer the bomb to another plane, Sweeney, after briefly conferring with Tibbets, decided to take off without further delay. It was now 2:45 a.m. and he was behind schedule. With *Bockcar's* powerful engines roaring, Sweeney rolled over to Runway A. Looking down the 8,500 foot runway he only saw

BOCK'S CAR co-pilot Fred Olivi, right, and crew members Spitzer and Van Pelt prepare for Nagasaki mission on Tinain's North Field, August 9, 1945. U.S. Army Photo.

inky darkness. Surprisingly, the spotlight that always illuminated the end of the runway at the edge of the Pacific Ocean was turned off.

An awesome task faced Sweeney as he tried to get a 77 ½ ton airplane safely in the air, a 10 member crew (not counting three passengers), 7,000 tons of aviation fuel, and a 10,300 pound bomb. Unlike "Little Boy," this baby was already "wired" and ready to go. One misstep and *Bockscar*, its crew, and even Tinian itself would likely be vaporized into smithereens.

"Stand by for takeoff," Sweeney finally sang out at 2:56 a.m. Gradually he opened the throttle, released the brakes, rolled the great airplane forward, and picked up momentum down the dark runway. At the last possible moment he launched skyward only a few feet above the water.

Where the flight of the *Enola Gay* was carried out with clockwork precision, *Bockscar's* lonely saga was beset with a myriad of problems from the outset. Turbulent weather forced Sweeney to go up to 17,000 feet then to 30,000 feet for an expected rendezvous with a trailing B-29 over Yakoshima at 7:45 a.m. More time and fuel were lost when the other aircraft failed to arrive. After circling the area for several valuable minutes, Sweeney finally broke off and headed for Kokura. Though the cloud cover was quite pervasive

Bock's Car crew shortly after returning to Tinian. L. to R. Bottom row-Kuharek, Spitzer, Gallagher, Buckley, Dehart. Top row-Sweeney, Asbury, Olivi, Beahan, Van Pelt, Beser.

over the city, he had already started his bomb run at 9:45 when bombardier Kermit Beahan shouted: "I can't see it! Smoke is obscuring the target." One more run produced the same result.

Time was now a critical factor, so Sweeney abruptly changed course and headed over to Nagasaki, the secondary target. To his dismay, he found that area obscured by 80 to 90 per cent cumulus clouds. With only enough fuel left to make one bomb run, Sweeney got a miracle of sorts when the clouds partially melted away and the target appeared in Beahan's bomb sight. He called out "Bomb away" and "Fat Boy" broke loose to begin its long journey to ground zero.

With the airplane now 10,000 pounds lighter, *Bockscar* lurched forward. Sweeney went into a sharp, diving 155-degree turn to the left in a northeasterly direction to get as far away as possible from the blast site. Within moments the entire horizon exploded into a super brilliant white with an intense flash that was much brighter than the one at Hiroshima. The light that illuminated the heavens was blinding. A moment later and the first wave of superheated air began pounding *Bockscar*. Over Hiroshima there were four or five similar shock waves of diminishing force, but these kept coming one after another with equal impact, perhaps five in all he thought.

As Sweeney completed his turn, he could see a brownish horizontal cloud encircling the stricken city. Brownish bile soaring upward toward *Bockscar* was more intense and angry than anything seen at Hiroshima. At about 25,000 feet the mushroom cloud broke off, sped passed the aircraft at 30,000 feet, and shot on up to at least 45,000 feet.

As things quieted down, the crew breathed a heavy sigh of relief; it was time to head home.

More problems were coming. Only 300 gallons of fuel remained in *Bockscar's* tanks, not nearly enough to get the aircraft back to Tinian. A secondary landing strip must be found or Sweeney would have to dump in the ocean. Okinawa was the most likely spot since it was only 350 miles away. He thought he could make it—but barely!

After what seemed like an eternity, Okinawa's airport appeared in the distance. Seeing heavy traffic arriving and departing on the landing strip, Sweeney urgently radioed "May Day, May Day" to the tower. Long moments passed before the runways finally started clearing to avoid what appeared to be a crash landing by a mysterious aircraft not slated to land there. Coming in barely on fumes, Sweeney sharply descended, hit the pavement at 140 mph, bounced about 25 feet into the air, came down, and veered sharply to the left toward a line of airplanes. An imminent collision was avoided when *Bockscar* abruptly slowed down to a roll and coasted over to the side of the runway.

After grabbing a bite to eat and relaxing a bit, the crew was airborne again two hours later headed for Tinian and home five hours away. At 10:30 p.m., 20 hours from his take-off, Sweeney finally set the aircraft down on Runway A. In contrast to the *Enola Gay's* return, only a few people turned out to welcome the men who bombed Nagasaki: Paul Tibbets, the ground crew, and a photographer. No matter! The relieved crew was just grateful to be safely home.

Though Sweeney's flight was understandably overshadowed by the earlier mission of the *Enola Gay*, it deserves more than a postscript in history. Convinced by the Nagasaki bombing that further resistance was futile, the Emperor directly involved himself in the surrender negotiations then underway. On August 14, he announced that Japan would surrender unconditionally, the first time ordinary Japanese citizens had ever heard his voice.

When word that the war was over reached Okinawa, where so much American blood had been shed, unrestrained celebrations broke out among the troops there. The long expected invasion of the Japanese mainland would never come. In other parts of the world, American soldiers, awaiting their transfer to the Pacific, were also overcome with unrestrained joy. One of them later reflected: "We were going to grow to adulthood after all."

On June 28, 1946, Sweeney was discharged from active duty with the rank of Lieutenant- Colonel.

Back home after her bumpy mission, Bock's Car rests on Tinian tarmac.

His military service awards include: Silver Star; Air Medal; Asiatic-Pacific Service Medal with two bronze stars; World War II Victory Medal; Occupation of Japan Medal; and Armed Forces Reserve Medal. In the post-war years he rose to the rank of major-general in the Massachusetts National Guard.

General Sweeney died on July 19, 2004, in Milton, Massachusetts.

As for *Bockscar*, that hardy, never quit airplane, reposes in quiet dignity in the United States Air Force Museum in Dayton, Ohio, where it, like the *Enola Gay* near Washington, is seen by thousands of admiring visitors each year.

Major Sweeney is awarded Air Medal by General Davies for successfully completing the Nagasaki mission.
He also received the Silver Star.

Selected Bibliography

Books

Astor, Gerald. *Semper Fi in the Sky: The Marine Air Battles of World War II*. New York: Ballentine Books, 2005.

Bernstein, Barton J. and Matusow, Allen J., Editors. *The Truman Administration: A Documentary History*. New York: Harper & Row, 1966.

Boyington, Gregory "Pappy." *Baa Baa Black Sheep*. New York, Bantom Books, 1958.

Boyne, Walter J. *Clash of Titans: World War II at Sea*. New York: Simon & Shuster, 1995.

Bradley, James. *Flyboys: A True Story of Courage*. New York: Little, Brown and Company, 2003.

Costello, John. *The Pacific War*. New York: Rawson, Wade Publishers Inc., 1981.

Davis, Donald. *Lightning Strike: The Secret Mission to Kill Admiral Yamamoto and Avenge Pearl Harbor*. New York: St. Martin's Press, 2005.

DeGroot, Gerard J. *The Bomb: A Life*. Cambridge, Massachusetts: Harvard University Press, 2005.

Donovan, Robert J. *Conflict and Crisis: The Presidency of Harry S. Truman, 1945-1948*. New York: W.W. Norton & Company, 1977.

Gamble, Bruce. *Black Sheep One: The Life of Gregory "Pappy" Boyington*. Novota, California, 2000.

Glines, Carroll V. *Attack On Yamamoto*. New York: Orion Books, 1990.

Groom, Winston. *1942: The Year That Tried Men's Souls*. New York: Grove Press, 2005.

Hoyt, Edwin P. *How They Won the War in the Pacific: Nimitz and His Admirals*. New York: Weybright and Talley, 1970.

Hymas, Joe. *Flight of the Avenger: George Bush at War*. New York: Harcourt Brace Jovanovich, Publishers, 1991.

Lawson, Captain Ted and Considine, Robert, Editor. *Thirty Seconds Over Tokyo*. New York: Pocket Star Books (Reprint), 2002.

Layton, Rear Admiral Edwin T., U.S.N. (Ret.). *And I Was There: Pearl Harbor and Midway—Breaking the Secrets*. New York: William Morrow and Company, Inc., 1985.

McCullough, David. *Truman*. New York: Simon & Shuster, 1992.

Mee, Jr., Charles L. *Meeting at Potsdam*. New York: M. Evans & Company, 1975.

Marston, Daniel, Editor. *The Pacific War Companion: From Pearl Harbor to Hiroshima*. Great Britain: Osprey Publishing, 2007.

Nelson, Craig. *The First Heroes: The Extraordinary Story of the Doolittle Raid—America's First World War II Victory*. New York: Viking, 2002.

Newcomb, Richard F., *Abandon Ship: The Saga of the U.S.S. Indianapolis, the Navy's Greatest Sea Disaster*. New York: Harper Collins, Publishers, 2001.

Roleff, Tamara L., Editor. *The Atom Bomb*. San Diego, CA: Greenhaven Press, Inc., 2000.

Schom, Alan. *The Eagle and the Rising Sun. The Japanese-American War, 1941-1943*. New York: W.W. Norton & Company, 2004.

Spector, Ronald H. *Eagle Against the Sun: The American War With Japan*. New York: The Free Press, 1985.

Stanton, Doug. *In Harm's Way: The Sinking of the USS Indianapolis and the Extraordinary Story of Its Survivors.* New York: MJF Books, 2001.

Sweeney, Maj. Gen. Charles W. Sweeney, U.S.A.F. (Ret.) with James A. Antonucci and Marion K. Antonucci. *War's End: An Eyewitness Account of America's Last Atomic Mission.* New York: Avon Books, 1997.

Thomas, Gordon. *Enola Gay: The Bombing of Hiroshima.* Old Saybrook, CT: Konecky & Konecky, 1977.

Tibbets, Brig. Gen. and Gerry Newhouse, *The 509th Composite Group History.* Columbus, OH: Mid-Coast Marketing, 2002 (Reprint of 1945 edition).

Walker, Stephen. *Shockwave: Countdown to Hiroshima.* New York: Harper Collins Publishers, 2005.

Warren, James A. *American Spartans: The U.S. Marines: A combat History from Iwo Jima to Iraq.* New York: The Free Press, 2005.

Watson, C. Hoyt. *The Amazing Story of Sergeant Jacob DeShazer.* (2002 Reprint) Originally published Winona Lake, Indiana: Light and Life Press.

Webster, Donovan. *The Burma Road: The Epic Story of the China-Burma-India Theater in World War II.* New York: Farrar, Straus and Giroux, 2003.

"World War II Times," Various Issues

Personal correspondence and interviews

President George H.W. Bush

General Paul Tibbets, Jr.

Alex Vraciu

Raymond "Hap" Halloran

Adrian Marks

Dr. Robert Palmer